CHURCHILL AT WAR

Churchill At War
His 'Finest Hour' in Photographs 1940-1945

Text copyright © 2003 by Martin Gilbert
Design copyright © 2003 by Carlton Books Limited
First American edition 2004
All rights reserved
Printed and bound in Italy

Layout design: Simon Mercer

ISBN: 0-393-05878-6

Originally published in Great Britain by
Carlton Books Limited 2003

W.W. Norton & Company, Inc.
500 Fifth Avenue, New York, NY 10110
www.wwnorton.com

W.W. Norton & Company Ltd.,
Castle House, 75/76 Wells Street, London W1T 3QT

1 2 3 4 5 6 7 8 9 0

IMPERIAL WAR
MUSEUM

MARTIN GILBERT
CHURCHILL
AT WAR

HIS 'FINEST HOUR' IN PHOTOGRAPHS
1940-1945

W · W · NORTON

NEW YORK · LONDON

C O N T E N T S

1940   BRITAIN AT BAY   6

1941   BRITAIN ALONE   22

1942   FIGHTING BACK   68

1943   THE TURN OF THE TIDE   82

1944   THE DRIVE TO VICTORY   110

1945   THE WAR IS WON   138

INDEX   158

ACKNOWLEDGEMENTS   160

OPPOSITE Churchill greeted by thousands of victorious British troops, North Africa, 1 June 1943.

1940

BRITAIN AT BAY

ON 10 MAY 1940, German forces attacked France, Belgium and Holland, in a sudden and unexpected onslaught. That morning, the Prime Minister, Neville Chamberlain, was certain that, because of the dramatic turn of events, he would have to remain at the helm, despite the growing unrest against his leadership. But both the Labour Party – then in opposition – and many leading Conservatives, who had hitherto been Chamberlain's supporters, felt that only Winston Churchill could give effective leadership, irrespective of Party or class.

Intense political discussions took place throughout the morning of 10 May, interspersed with meetings to discuss the military crisis in Europe, a crisis that worsened by the hour, as German forces drove deeper and deeper into Belgium, Holland and France. By midday, Chamberlain had been told by his closest Conservative allies that a new Prime Minister was needed – a new hand on the helm – a man of proven determination, capable of inspiring public confidence. Churchill had all this, as well as experience of high office in the First World War.

Chamberlain's instinct, confronted by the extraordinary dangers of the German military onslaught, was to remain at Downing Street in order to see the crisis through. But as the day unfolded with its worsening catalogue of news from the battle zones, many leading politicians were insisting that a coalition government made up of all political Parties was essential to deal with the crisis. Chamberlain agreed, and was prepared to lead an all-Party administration, but the Labour Party refused to serve under him.

The choice fell on Churchill. By the evening of 10 May, having gone to Buckingham Palace to see King George VI, he became Prime Minister, chosen to lead the nation in its new time of trial. He was sixty-five years old. He later recalled: "As I went to bed at about 3 a.m. I was conscious of a profound sense of relief. At last I had authority to give directions over the whole scene. I felt as if I were walking with destiny, and that all my past life had been but a preparation for this hour and for this trial."

The eight months that followed, until the end of 1940, were testing times for Britain, and for Churchill. He knew how ill-prepared Britain was to face a German invasion, and he watched with alarm as Holland surrendered to the Germans on 14 May and the Belgians capitulated two weeks later, whereupon Germany turned its military and air power against France. With the evacuation of the British Expeditionary Force from Dunkirk, and the French surrender, it seemed that only a few weeks were needed before Hitler sent an army across the English Channel. Churchill was at the centre of the national effort – which he inspired with his speeches and his presence – to try to prepare for the imminent arrival of German troops on British soil. They never came. Hitler decided instead to defeat Britain in the air before risking an invasion.

The air battle was intense. Churchill reflected the mood of the whole country when he said of the airmen who defended the skies above Britain against enormous odds: "Never in the field of human conflict has so much been owed by so many to so few." Then the German Air Force turned its energies and power to the bombing of London and other British cities. Tens of thousands of civilians were killed, and large areas of docklands, factories and private homes laid waste.

Churchill's speeches breathed defiance and confidence. But he never minimized the dangers. In a broadcast on 11 September 1940, as German bombers were wreaking havoc in London, and the British were wondering how such a ferocious onslaught would end, he spoke of "a people who will not flinch or weary of the struggle – hard and protracted though it will be".

Behind the scenes, Churchill worked with extraordinary energy and intensity to improve Britain's defences and to build up the armaments and forces needed to repel an invasion if it came, to fight in North Africa against the Italian forces that were seeking to drive the British from Egypt, and to control the Suez Canal – Britain's eastern supply lifeline.

The Atlantic lifeline was also under intense threat, as German submarines sank more and more of the merchant ships on which Britain depended for its food and arms supplies. One of Churchill's principal tasks throughout his Premiership, but particularly during its first months, was to persuade the American President, Franklin Delano Roosevelt, to allow Britain to purchase the war supplies on the scale needed for Britain to be able to resist a German invasion, or carry on the war until it could be taken to Europe.

LEFT Churchill on the day he became Prime Minister, 10 May 1940, following a meeting of the War Cabinet, waves at a small crowd that had gathered outside 10 Downing Street.

LEFT France having signed an armistice with Germany on 22 June, Britain awaited a German invasion. On 14 July 1940, Churchill inspected the defences in southern England, including a heavy-gun emplacement.

RIGHT Also on 14 July, Churchill inspected a brick blockhouse that was being built, and lent a hand in laying a course of bricks. Ten years earlier he had built a wall and a cottage on his country estate, at Chartwell in Kent, and had become a member of the Bricklayers' Union.

LEFT Churchill leaves the blockhouse.

OVERLEAF Churchill leads a group of officers – and his two detectives in plain clothes – on an inspection of the South Coast defences, 31 July 1940.

On 31 July 1940 Churchill inspected the coastal fortifications and defence works. He is seen here on a sandbagged gun emplacement, with its defenders.

As the Germans contemplated invading Britain, they embarked on a
massive bombing campaign of the coastal towns that they would have to
overrun if they were to advance inland. On 28 August 1940, Churchill
visited Dover and Ramsgate, both of which had just been heavily bombed.
While he was in Ramsgate, there was an almost continuous air raid
warning, but he carried on with his inspection. At one point he witnessed
an air battle in which two German aircraft were shot down.

LEFT Churchill visits a bed and
breakfast hotel in Ramsgate.
The building had been bombed
a short while earlier. Partly masked
by Churchill's hat is his son-in-law
Duncan Sandys, Churchill's Special
Liaison Officer with Home Defence
and Air Raid Precautions. Emerging
from the doorway is Major General
Hastings Ismay, the head of
Churchill's Defence Staff and one
of his closest wartime colleagues.

RIGHT Churchill leaves the air raid
shelter tunnels at Ramsgate.
Immediately behind him, also
wearing a steel helmet, is his son-in-
law Duncan Sandys.

ABOVE At Dover, Churchill studies reports of the action that day with
Vice Admiral Sir Bertram Ramsay, Flag Officer Commanding Dover, who
was in charge of the naval defences of the Dover Strait.

OPPOSITE While he was in Dover on 28 August 1940, Churchill and General Ismay (on the left) put on their steel helmets and, from a position above the docks, watched through binoculars as British and German pilots fought in the skies above the English Channel.

BELOW Churchill pauses for a moment while visiting the defences of Dover.

ABOVE To meet the threat of a German invasion, troops from Canada, Australia and New Zealand were rushed to Britain by sea. On 9 September 1940, Churchill visited a camp of Australian troops, and joined in the singing. On the left, in officer's uniform, Duncan Sandys observes his father-in-law.

RIGHT On the morning of 13 September 1940, German bombs fell on Buckingham Palace. A few hours later, Churchill visited the Palace to see the damage. During his visit he was photographed with Queen Elizabeth and King George VI.

RIGHT As the German bombing of London intensified, the docks were hit again and again. On 25 September 1940, following a particularly severe air raid, Churchill inspected the damage by boat. He travelled along the River Thames with his wife Clementine; both were visibly shocked by the extent of the destruction.

LEFT As Churchill travelled down the Thames, a ferryboat passed: while the passengers cheered, Churchill raised his hat in acknowledgement.

OPPOSITE On 23 October 1940, after a visit to Scotland, where he inspected troops and coastal fortifications, Churchill was reading while waiting for his train at St Andrews Station, when two photographers snapped him – the photographer who took this picture, and a soldier on the platform (observed by a schoolboy).

RIGHT On the night of 29–30 December 1940, the Germans launched one of their heaviest raids of the war on London. Enormous destruction was caused. The following morning Churchill and Clementine inspected the damage. They are seen here at the Guildhall, one of London's finest medieval buildings, which was almost entirely destroyed. In the years before the war, Churchill had spoken there several times at official banquets, amid much splendour and ceremony.

LEFT As Churchill walked with his wife through the bomb-damaged streets that day, he was followed by a crowd of Londoners. He was devastated by the destruction he saw. On the far right in the photograph (without a hat) is his friend and Parliamentary Private Secretary, Brendan Bracken.

Churchill leaves the flagship of Admiral John Tovey, Commander-in-Chief, Home Fleet in January 1941.

1941
BRITAIN ALONE

THE YEAR 1941 was to be one of considerable travel for Churchill. The photograph opposite shows him at a Scottish port, leaving a battleship to return to shore.

A moment of great relief for Churchill came on 11 March when President Roosevelt signed the Lend-Lease Act, under which Britain could loan vital war materials for as long as the war might last. Churchill called Lend-Lease "the most unselfish and unsordid financial act of any country in all history". By the end of the war, the United States had provided Britain with half its tanks, most of its transport aircraft, a quarter of its ammunition, and almost all its extra shipping needs as the German U-boats continued to wreak havoc on British merchant shipping.

The war at sea was a source of grave concern for Churchill throughout 1941. The heavy loss of life, both among sailors of the Royal Navy and merchant seamen, caused him great anxiety. So too did the continuing German bombing of British cities. Churchill made many visits to the scenes of destruction. His presence inspired those whose lives had been made a torment. Following his visit to Bristol on the morning after a heavy air raid, he was in tears when he saw the extent of the damage, but the fact that he was there gave people courage. After the Bristol visit, General Ismay, the head of his Defence Staff, wrote to him of how, at one of the rest centres for those whose homes had been destroyed, "there was a poor old woman who had lost all her belongings, sobbing her heart out. But as you entered, she took her handkerchief from her eyes and waved it madly, shouting 'Hooray, hooray'."

Churchill's meeting with Roosevelt that year, on board ship off the coast of Newfoundland, was a turning point in Churchill's direction of the war, opening out the possibility of ever greater support from the leader of a country that was still neutral. As a result of the relationship that had developed between the two leaders, the United States war arsenal was put increasingly at the support of Britain. After his first meeting with Roosevelt, Churchill told the Lord Privy Seal, Clement Attlee – the Leader of the Labour Party, who was later to be Churchill's Deputy Prime Minister – "I am sure I have established warm and deep personal relations with our great friend."

It was during Divine Service on board that a sense of common purpose emerged most strongly. Churchill had chosen the hymns: "For those in Peril on the Sea", "O God our Help in Ages Past", "Onward Christian Soldiers" and "Eternal Father Strong to Save". Later he recalled: "The service was felt by us all to be a deeply moving expression of the unity of faith of our two peoples, and none who took part in it will forget the spectacle presented that sunlit morning on the crowded quarterdeck – the symbolism of the Union Jack and Stars and Stripes draped side by side on the pulpit…"

A culminating point of this first meeting between Prime Minister and President was the Atlantic Charter. For the next half century it remained a beacon of hope for peoples in bondage. Britain and the United States pledged themselves to "respect the right of all peoples to choose the form of government under which they live; and they wish to see sovereign rights and self-government restored to those who have been forcibly deprived of them." The outcome of the war was to be different to that of 1914–18: the two countries pledged themselves to "no aggrandisement, territorial or other", as a result of the war. The people of all nations were to be entitled to "improved labour standards, economic advancement and social security".

These pledges depended for their European impact upon the defeat of Germany. When the Atlantic Charter was signed, the United States was still neutral, and German rule and tyranny were everywhere on the ascendant on the continent of Europe. Greece and Yugoslavia had been conquered in April and the Soviet Union faced the possibility of total annihilation. Central to Churchill's war direction in the last half of 1941 was his understanding that if Hitler overran the Soviet Union, he would gain vast extra resources to turn against Britain. From the earliest moments of the eastern war, Churchill therefore made every effort to provide the Soviet Union with whatever help Britain could assemble, including a whole month's worth of British tank production, 1,800 fighter planes, and the transhipment to Russian Arctic ports of munitions and aircraft. Churchill's wife Clementine headed an Aid to Russia Appeal that provided medical help on a substantial scale, including the equipment for several field hospitals.

On 7 December 1941, as the year drew to an end, Britain was attacked by Japan in the Far East. On the same day, Japan attacked the United States, striking without declaration of war or warning at Pearl Harbor. Four days later, Hitler declared war on the United States. "The accession of the United States makes amends for all", Churchill told his Foreign Secretary, Anthony Eden, "and with time and patience will give certain victory."

Britain and the United States were allies in the war with Germany. Churchill set off once more to see Roosevelt, and to coordinate their respective war strategies.

ABOVE Churchill greets Roosevelt's personal emissary, Harry Hopkins, at 10 Downing Street on 10 January 1941. Between them is Brendan Bracken, who was one of Churchill's closest confidants.

OPPOSITE On a visit to Southampton and Portsmouth with Harry Hopkins, Churchill shakes hands with George Smith, aged sixteen, who was believed to be the youngest worker in the Portsmouth dockyard. Churchill is carrying his regulation gas mask, a service respirator as issued to the armed forces.

LEFT While in Portsmouth on 31 January 1941, Churchill inspected a unit of French sailors. They had responded to the call of the Free French leader, General Charles de Gaulle, to participate in the struggle against Nazism, despite the surrender of France and the establishment of a pro-German government under Marshal Pétain. Churchill is carrying his gas mask and helmet. Behind Churchill is Harry Hopkins, and to Hopkins' left, General Ismay.

ABOVE On 4 February 1941 Churchill inspected British armoured units. On his left is General de Gaulle, and on his right the leader of the Polish forces, General Wladyslaw Sikorski. Both France and Poland had been defeated by Germany, but both nations found military leaders willing to fight on, and to form forces in exile with a view to participating in the war then being fought in North Africa, and in due course in Italy and north-west Europe.

ABOVE Lifting his hat on his cane, Churchill drives through the streets of Bristol on 12 April 1941, after a severe air raid the previous night.

RIGHT At a bombed building in Bristol, Churchill shakes his fist defiantly, telling the onlookers: "We shall give it to them back." Immediately behind him (without a hat) is the American Ambassador to Britain, Gilbert Winant. Immediately behind Winant is Clementine Churchill, and in the foreground (leaning slightly backwards) is Churchill's detective, Inspector Walter Thompson, who travelled with him throughout the war, both within Britain and abroad.

ABOVE Eight days after his visit to Bristol, Churchill inspects Czechoslovak troops training in England. Their country, like France and Poland, had been overrun by Germany, but their leaders, including Eduard Beneš, President of the Czechoslovak government-in-exile (standing with Churchill), were determined to fight alongside Britain until their country was liberated.

ABOVE An air raid on Manchester on 28 April 1941 caused extensive destruction. On the following day Churchill and his wife visited the city.

RIGHT Churchill in Manchester on 29 April 1941. He called out to the onlookers, "Are we downhearted?" and they chorused back at him – "No!"

ABOVE Churchill amid the ruins of the Free Trade Hall, Manchester. "I made speeches here forty years ago", he commented. Those speeches were clarion calls for social reform, and a better life for the masses.

ABOVE Several German air raids on Plymouth at the end of April 1941 caused considerable damage to the docks and the town. Churchill visited the city on 2 May 1941. Onlookers saw him cry as he walked through the bombed streets. The woman behind Churchill is Nancy Astor, the Member of Parliament for Plymouth, who, in 1919, was the first woman to take her seat in the House of Commons.

OPPOSITE While in Plymouth on 2 May 1941, Churchill visited a naval establishment where work had continued despite the bombardment. With him was Averell Harriman, a special envoy from President Roosevelt, who had full authority to acquire from the United States the war-making materials urgently needed by Britain.

LEFT Visiting a British airfield on 6 June 1941, Churchill sat at the controls of a recently arrived American warplane, the Boeing B17 Flying Fortress.

BELOW During his visit, Churchill inspected the crew of a British Wellington bomber.

OPPOSITE American war equipment, including aeroplanes, tanks and guns, reached Britain in ever-increasing quantities during the summer of 1941. As Churchill told the House of Commons, an American Catalina seaplane had played an important part in hunting down the German warship *Bismarck*. Here, on 23 May 1941, Churchill inspects an American General Grant tank.

ABOVE American military aid was essential to enable Britain to carry on the war. During his visit to a bomber station on 6 June 1941, Churchill watches a Flying Fortress. These American aircraft were providing essential strength to Britain's growing bomber offensive against German factories, and military, naval and airforce installations.

ABOVE On 13 June 1941, watched by the Secretary of State for War, David Margesson (in bowler hat), and Inspector Thompson (on his left), Churchill test fires a new automatic gun.

ABOVE Churchill working during a journey by train to the south-east
of England on 20 June 1941. Although not visible in the photograph,
his secretary, Kathleen Hill, is seated opposite him. She would take
dictation on a special "silent" model of typewriter as he spoke. In front of
him, on the table, is a page of the speech notes which Mrs Hill had typed
out. The censor has scratched them out on the negative.

ABOVE During his visit to the south-east on 20 June 1941, Churchill inspected HMG *Boche Buster*, one of Britain's largest heavy guns, which could fire from a railway siding. His detective, Inspector Thompson, awaits him on the track.

LEFT Crowds surround Churchill as he walks through Whitehall, on his way to the National Liberal Club for the ceremonial unveiling of a portrait of himself.

ABOVE Churchill at a banquet in the Mansion House, a few moments before speaking. At a time when the Germans were masters of Europe, and the sinking of British merchant ships was continuous, Churchill's public speeches were powerful appeals for national unity and perseverance.

ABOVE During a tour of inspection on 22 July 1941, Churchill entered the
turret of a new British tank, a heavy infantry tank with a six-pounder gun.
The tank had been given the name "Churchill". It was so strongly armoured
that it could be used as a defensive pillbox. Churchill, wearing a beret of the
Royal Tank Regiment, is talking by wireless telephone to the tank's driver.

ABOVE During a visit to Southern Command on 25 July 1941, Churchill saw a mock battle during which live ammunition was fired. The binoculars that he wore were a gift from Admiral Sims, who had used them when commanding the American Fleet in European waters during the First World War.

LEFT August 1941. General Ismay, the head of Churchill's Defence Office, photographs Churchill on board the battleship HMS *Prince of Wales*. Churchill was on his way, together with the British Chiefs of Staff, to Argentia Bay off Newfoundland, for his first meeting with President Roosevelt. On the far right, with a cigarette, is Roosevelt's emissary Harry Hopkins. Churchill is with the Chief of the Naval Staff, Admiral Pound (next to him), and the commander of *Prince of Wales*, Captain Leach.

LEFT On board *Prince of Wales*, Churchill confers with three of his senior advisers, Admiral Pound (left), General Sir John Dill (Chief of the Imperial General Staff), and, on the right of the picture, Air Chief Marshal Sir Wilfrid Freeman (Vice Chief of the Air Staff).

OPPOSITE Churchill, with Lord Beaverbrook, then Minister of Supply. Beaverbrook, a Canadian-born newspaper proprietor, had been a friend of Churchill's since before the First World War.

ABOVE Reaching *Augusta*, on 9 August 1941, Churchill hands Roosevelt a letter from King George VI. It was the first meeting between Prime Minister and President since they had met, briefly, at a banquet in Britain during the First World War, when Roosevelt was Assistant Secretary of the Navy, and Churchill was Minister of Munitions. Somewhat to Roosevelt's chagrin, Churchill had no recollection of this meeting. Roosevelt, a victim of polio, is holding on to the arm of one of his sons, Elliott. The civilian looking on is Sir Alexander Cadogan, head of the British Foreign Office

OPPOSITE Churchill and Lord Beaverbrook leave *Prince of Wales* for the boat that will take them to President Roosevelt, who was on board the American cruiser *Augusta*.

LEFT Roosevelt and Churchill at Divine Service on board *Prince of Wales*, 10 August 1941. British and American leaders and sailors join in the hymns, which Churchill had chosen.

RIGHT Roosevelt and Churchill in conversation after Divine Service on *Prince of Wales*. In the background, just behind Roosevelt, wearing a borrowed naval cap, is Churchill's Principal Private Secretary, John Martin. On the right of the picture is Roosevelt's special envoy to Britain, Averell Harriman.

BELOW As *Augusta* steams away, taking Roosevelt back to the United States, Churchill watches it depart from the deck of *Prince of Wales*.

BELOW Returning to Britain on board *Prince of Wales*, Churchill strokes the ship's cat, Blackie. Within four months the ship had been sunk by the Japanese off the coast of Malaya, with the loss of half its officers and men.

LEFT On his return from meeting Roosevelt off Newfoundland, Churchill visited Iceland, which was under joint British and American occupation. Here he is seen inspecting American Marines. Immediately behind him in naval uniform is Roosevelt's son, Franklin Roosevelt Jr, who travelled with him to Iceland. While there, Churchill promised the Icelanders that when the war was won their island would obtain its independence from Denmark.

RIGHT As he leaves Iceland, Churchill gives a passing ship his "V-for-Victory" sign. Behind him is his naval aide-de-camp, Lieutenant Commander C.R. "Tommy" Thompson, who accompanied him on all his wartime journeys.

OPPOSITE Reaching London after his transatlantic journey, Churchill is greeted by Clement Attlee, Lord Privy Seal and leader of the Labour Party. Attlee had fought at Gallipoli in the First World War, and regarded that campaign as an inspired attempt by Churchill to shorten the war.

OPPOSITE Churchill leaves Downing Street for Buckingham Palace, to take King George VI a letter from the President. Churchill is talking to his Principal Private Secretary, John Martin, who had accompanied him on the transatlantic journey. Behind them is Inspector Thompson.

ABOVE On 25 September 1941 Churchill visits No. 615 Fighter Squadron, of which he had been Honorary Air Commodore since before the war. Here, wearing his Air Commodore's uniform, Churchill talks to the pilots.

LEFT Churchill and his wife, with the commanding officer of 615 Squadron. Behind them is Jock Colville, Churchill's Junior Private Secretary, who was about to leave Churchill's staff to join the Royal Air Force. He returned later in the war, and, during Churchill's second premiership (1951–55), served as Churchill's Joint Principal Private Secretary.

LEFT By September 1941, Britain had endured a year of German bombing, and more than 30,000 civilians had been killed. On 28 September Churchill visited Coventry, which had been severely bombed a year earlier, when 507 civilians had been killed. Here he walks amid the ruins of Coventry Cathedral.

RIGHT During his visit to an aeroplane factory in Coventry, Churchill watches a woman riveter at work on a Spitfire.

ABOVE In Birmingham, watched by children and adults perched on a bomb-damaged wall, Churchill greets Air Raid Precautions (ARP) workers.

RIGHT During his tour of bomb-damaged cities on 28 and 29 September 1941, Churchill also watched a demonstration flight in a Spitfire by the test pilot Alex Henshaw. Here he talks to the pilot about the flight. Before the war Henshaw had won the flight record for Cape Town to London.

BELOW Visiting Liverpool, which had been badly bombed, Churchill talks to two dock workers. "Are you managing to get plenty of food?" he asked them. "Aye sir, we're doing grand, thank you", was their reply.

ABOVE The citizens of bomb-damaged Liverpool cheer Churchill.

ABOVE The War Cabinet, photographed in the garden of 10 Downing Street in October 1941. Back row, left to right: Arthur Greenwood, Minister without Portfolio; Ernest Bevin, Minister of Labour; Lord Beaverbrook, Minister of Supply; and Sir Kingsley Wood, Chancellor of the Exchequer (one of the leading Conservatives who, on 10 May 1940, had insisted that Churchill became Prime Minister). Bottom row, left to right: Sir John Anderson, Lord President of the Council, with secret responsibility for the development of the atomic bomb; Churchill; Clement Attlee, Lord Privy Seal (soon to be Deputy Prime Minister) and Anthony Eden, Foreign Secretary.

ABOVE In December 1941 Clementine Churchill launched her Red Cross Aid to Russia Appeal, which provided medicine and equipment for military hospitals throughout the Soviet Union, including a million doses of the most recent pain killer. The first person to make a donation and receive an emblem for his lapel was her husband, seen here handing her a banknote. The photograph was issued to the British newspapers on 16 December 1941, for immediate publication. Churchill had in fact left Britain on 13 December by sea for the United States. The photograph was deliberately issued while he was on his journey, as part of the deception plan to keep his travel secret, and make the Germans believe he was still in Britain.

OPPOSITE On 13 December 1941, six days after the Japanese attack on the United States at Pearl Harbor, and on Britain in Hong Kong and Malaya, Churchill set off across the Atlantic to visit President Roosevelt for the second time in the war. He made the crossing on the battleship *Duke of York*. Here he salutes his daughter Mary, then a lance corporal in the Auxiliary Territorial Service (ATS), in which Princess Elizabeth also served. Mary had gone on board to wish her father "Godspeed".

ABOVE Churchill walks on the deck of the *Duke of York* with his Personal Secretary, Kathleen Hill, who had joined him as his first resident secretary in 1936, and who remained at his side until the end of the war. Her discretion was absolute, and her mastery of Churchill's working methods was total. Behind Churchill and Mrs Hill are Averell Harriman, Roosevelt's special envoy, and Mary Churchill.

OPPOSITE, ABOVE AND RIGHT
Churchill in the garden of the White House, Washington, December 1941. Behind him, in the photograph opposite, is Harry Hopkins. Churchill is wearing what he called "my siren suit", a one-piece garment with a zip fastener. The siren suit had a particular advantage, it could be put on in one minute. It quickly became Churchill's favourite garb. At a press conference that week Mrs Roosevelt announced that she was having a similar suit made for her husband.

LEFT On 26 December 1941, Churchill addressed a joint session of the United States Congress, telling the Senators and Congressmen "If my father had been American and my mother British, instead of the other way round, I might have got here on my own." On the rostrum behind him is (left) the acting Speaker, Representative William P. Cole Jr, of Maryland, and (right) Vice President Henry A. Wallace. At the lower left is the Senate Majority Leader, Alben W. Barkley, from Kentucky.

BELOW From Washington, Churchill travelled to the Canadian capital, Ottawa. Here, in front of Government House, he inspects Canadian Naval Cadets.

RIGHT AND BELOW On 30 December 1941, while in Ottawa, Churchill addressed Canadian Parliamentarians. His speech was broadcast through the microphones of the Canadian Broadcasting Corporation. Churchill told the Parliamentarians, and the world, that when Hitler had been preparing to invade Britain in the summer of 1940, the French generals, in Churchill's words, "had told their Prime Minister and his divided Cabinet that 'In three weeks, England will have her neck wrung like a chicken'." Churchill commented: "Some chicken!" – and then added, to the Parliamentarians' laughter, "some neck!"

On his return to Britain from the United States in January 1942, Churchill went by ship to Bermuda, and then by flying boat to Britain. During the flight, wearing his comfortable siren suit, he chatted to the pilot, Commander Kelly Rogers.

1942

FIGHTING BACK

CHURCHILL SPENT CHRISTMAS 1941 and the early weeks of 1942 at the White House. This enabled him to work out a global war strategy with President Roosevelt, a strategy that, much to Churchill's relief, made the Anglo-American joint aim the defeat of Germany before the defeat of Japan.

While he was at the White House, Churchill suffered a mild heart attack. Nevertheless, two days later he made the long train journey to the Canadian capital, Ottawa, for talks with the Canadian government, and to address the Canadian Parliament. On his return to the United States – he was in the train travelling through the night when 1941 turned to 1942 – he went to Florida to recuperate, travelling incognito. He then returned to Washington for more talks with Roosevelt. Churchill's stamina was extraordinary.

Roosevelt's last words to Churchill as the Prime Minister set off for Britain were: "Trust me to the bitter end". In the event, Roosevelt died three and a half weeks before the German surrender. The two men were to have many disagreements of emphasis and direction, but their mutual respect and adherence to the common cause was total. Returning to Britain on 17 January 1942, Churchill told King George VI that Britain and the United States were now "married" after many months of "walking out".

In the Far East, Japan advanced remorselessly against the British, American and Dutch forces. The sinking of *Prince of Wales* (on which Churchill had travelled to see Roosevelt in the autumn of 1941), and of *Repulse*, with heavy loss of life were bitter blows, as was the fall of Hong Kong and Singapore. "When I reflect how I have longed and prayed for the entry of the United States into the war," Churchill confided in Roosevelt, "I find it difficult to realize how gravely our British affairs have deteriorated since December 7. We have suffered the greatest disaster of our history at Singapore, and other disasters will come thick and fast upon us." Churchill added: "Your great power will only become effective gradually because of the vast distances and the shortage of ships." But Churchill never allowed himself to despair, and it was Roosevelt who reminded him, when trying to console him over the recent setbacks: "This may be a critical period, but remember always it is not as bad as some you have so well survived before."

On the Eastern Front, Russia was struggling to prevent the Germans overrunning the Caucasus and reaching the oil fields of Baku. Churchill continued to send enormous amounts of military aid to the Soviet Union, but Stalin was emphatic that he wanted Britain and America to attack Germany in northern Europe before 1942 came to an end, and to open a "Second Front". After talks with Roosevelt, Churchill was deputed to fly to Moscow (in a vast arc via Cairo and Teheran, the only way possible) and to explain that neither country would have the resources to do so, particularly the requisite air superiority, for almost two years.

In the Western Desert, British and Commonwealth troops were battling with a German and Italian army led by Rommel, the "Desert Fox". When Rommel's forces overran the Allied garrison at Tobruk, Churchill was in Washington: the news was brought to him while he was talking to Roosevelt. The President immediately offered whatever reinforcements he could find, despite America's own desperate situation in the Pacific.

Slowly the advantage of war was turning in North Africa, where General Bernard Montgomery emerged as a scourge of the enemy. His victory over Rommel at El Alamein marked the beginning of the end of Axis control in Africa. On 8 November, substantial Anglo-American forces – Churchill's son Randolph was serving with them – landed on the North African coast. By the end of year the Germans were struggling to retain their last remaining strongholds in Tunisia, although still fighting, at Hitler's personal insistence, for every mile.

Fighting was fierce, and the advance was slow, and in the House of Commons there was unease at what seemed to Members of Parliament to be poor leadership. Hitler was still master of Europe. The seas were still the scene of persistent German submarine attacks and sinkings. On 11 November Churchill tried to put these criticisms in perspective, telling the parliamentarians: "How silly it is for people to imagine that governments can act on impulse or in immediate response to pressure in these large scale offensives. There must be planning, design and forethought, and after that a long period of silence which looks – I can quite understand it – to the ordinary spectator as if it were simply apathy or inertia, but which is in fact steady indispensable preparation for the blow."

Churchill was confident of victory, however long the struggle might be, and was buoyed up that Christmas by a message from Roosevelt – "The old team-work is grand."

LEFT Churchill, cigar in hand, sits in the co-pilot's seat of the flying boat returning him to Britain.

LEFT On 28 March 1942, Churchill spent a day among the troops of Southern Command. With him was the Turkish Ambassador, Rauf Orbay, whom Churchill was keen to impress with the fighting capacity of the British troops, hoping to deter Turkey from throwing in its lot with Germany. In the event, Turkey remained neutral until the last months of the war, when it declared war on Germany.

RIGHT During a visit to an anti-aircraft battery in Britain on 3 April 1942, having seen some soldiers bricklaying, Churchill asked them if they "had their tickets" in the Bricklayers' Union. He then said, "Here, let me lay one for you", and did so – as a member of the Bricklayers' Union since the 1920s.

BELOW LEFT Visiting a munitions factory on 15 May 1942, Churchill was presented with a cigar by one of the munitions workers, Miss Grace Stoddart.

BELOW RIGHT While walking around the munitions factory, Churchill had to obey the non-smoking regulations.

LEFT On 26 May 1942, Britain and the Soviet Union signed a twenty-year Treaty of Alliance and Mutual Assistance. After the signing, Churchill appeared for a celebratory photograph. From left to right: Ivan Maisky, the Soviet Ambassador to Britain; Vyacheslav Molotov, Soviet Commissar for Foreign Affairs (who had arrived in Britain six days earlier in a Soviet bomber); Clement Attlee, the Deputy Prime Minister; Oliver Lyttelton, Minister of Production (behind Churchill, in civilian clothes); Brigadier Roy Firebrace former Head of the British Military Mission to Moscow who was acting as an interpreter at this meeting (partially obscured, wearing glasses) and Anthony Eden, the Foreign Secretary.

BELOW Churchill returned to the United States for a meeting with Roosevelt in June 1942. Here he is seen at Camp Jackson in South Carolina, with General George C. Marshall, the Chief of the United States Army General Staff (left) and (on the right, with pith helmet) Henry Stimson, the American Secretary of War, watching a battalion of American paratroopers doing a parachute drop. Churchill later wrote: "I had never seen a thousand men leap into the air at once."

LEFT Even as substantial military supplies were being sent from Britain to the Soviet Union, including tanks and aircraft, Churchill flew to Moscow to discuss the joint war effort with the Soviet leader, Joseph Stalin. Here he is seen, on the morning of 13 August 1942, at an airport near Moscow, descending by ladder from the Liberator bomber that had flown him to the Soviet Union via the Middle East and Iran. It was the first time Churchill had set foot on Soviet soil.

RIGHT On arrival in Moscow, Churchill listens as a Russian band plays the Soviet and British anthems. An outspoken opponent of Communism since the Bolshevik Revolution of 1917, Churchill recognized that, with the German onslaught deep inside Russia, Britain and the Soviet Union had become essential allies in the defeat of Nazi tyranny, despite their conflicting ideologies, and that should the Soviet Union be defeated, Germany could hurl a vast victorious army, replete with its own enhanced oil resources, against Britain.

LEFT Churchill, Stalin, and Roosevelt's emissary Averell Harriman, meeting in the Kremlin on 16 August 1942. This photograph was transmitted to Britain by radio, hence its poor quality. Churchill had to disappoint Stalin by explaining to him that Britain and America would not be ready to invade continental Europe until 1944. Stalin had been pressing for such a "Second Front" in 1942. Britain's main effort, Churchill explained, would remain twofold: the bombing of German cities, and the fighting in the Western Desert against the German and Italian armies. At the same time, plans for the 1944 landings in north-west Europe would move steadily ahead.

OPPOSITE, BOTTOM On his way to Moscow, Churchill had visited the British and Commonwealth troops in the Western Desert, and on his return from Moscow he visited them again. Here, on 23 August 1942, he walks with the recently appointed General Officer Commanding the 8th Army, General Bernard Montgomery, in the army's forward area. Churchill has a tropical hat and holds an umbrella to keep off the sun. Montgomery is wearing an Australian Army hat. The officer walking several yards behind them is General Sir Alan Brooke, Chief of the Imperial General Staff.

ABOVE In the Western Desert, with General Sir Alan Brooke.

OVERLEAF Churchill watching a Churchill tank "somewhere in England": a photograph released to the newspapers on 19 September 1942. Five days earlier, Churchill had written to his eighty-three-year-old Aunt Leonie (Lady Leslie): "It seems to me that the tide of destiny is moving steadily in our favour, though our voyage will be long and rough."

RIGHT Military aid to the Soviet Union continued in even greater measure after Churchill's visit to Stalin. This aid had to travel by sea through the Arctic Ocean, and was subjected to repeated and often crippling German air and submarine attacks. On 13 October 1942, Churchill went on board one of the British warships that had just returned from northern Russia after escorting a convoy. Standing with him is Rear Admiral Robert Burnett, commanding the Home Fleet Destroyer Flotillas.

BELOW Churchill greets the commanding officers of the Royal Navy destroyers that had escorted the most recent convoy to Russia.

LEFT Churchill on board a battleship, 3 October 1942, during his visit to the Home Fleet after receiving the freedom of the City of Edinburgh. On the left is the Lord Privy Seal, Sir Stafford Cripps, a member of the War Cabinet. On 22 November Cripps left the War Cabinet to become Minister of Aircraft Production. During the First World War he had worked under Churchill at the Ministry of Munitions. Between the wars he had been a leading member of the Labour Party, from which he was expelled for his extreme left-wing socialist views. On the right is the Commander-in-Chief of the Home Fleet, Admiral Tovey. "Your presence with us," Tovey signalled to Churchill after the visit, "has been an encouragement and inspiration to us all."

RIGHT Churchill broadcasting news of the successful British offensive that had begun in the Western Desert on 23 October 1942. With the Battle of El Alamein, the German and Italian threat to Egypt was ended, and the tide of battle turned in the Western Desert.

ABOVE As 1942 came to an end, Churchill continued to visit troops in training in Britain. On 20 November, while watching infantry training in the South Eastern Area, and having seen a squad go over a battle course, he showed his own agility – ten days before his sixty-eighth birthday – by walking up one of the greased logs on the course, using his stick.

BELOW On 4 December 1942, Churchill visited a School of Infantry Training in the north of England. Here, with General Sir Bernard Paget, Commander-in-Chief of the Home Forces, he watches troops clambering over a wall.

Roosevelt and Churchill deep in conversation at the Casablanca Conference, Morocco, January 1943.

1 9 4 3

THE TURN OF THE TIDE

THE YEAR 1943 began with both Churchill and Roosevelt in Casablanca, for a conference that opened on 14 January, to decide on the strategy in each field of conflict, by land, sea and air, and in all the theatres of war, including Italy, northern Europe and the Far East. The two men also agreed that the Germans would not be allowed, as they had been in 1918, to agree to armistice terms, but would have to accept unconditional surrender.

In May, Churchill returned to Washington for talks with Roosevelt to coordinate Allied strategy. The two men also discussed the future of the atomic bomb, which was being developed in the United States with the participation of many British scientists, and together they initialled a solemn agreement not to use the new weapon against each other.

From Washington, Churchill flew direct to North Africa, where, in June, at Algiers, he presided over a series of discussions with senior British and American generals during which plans were finalized for the invasion of Sicily and Italy. In the Roman amphitheatre at Carthage, Churchill addressed a vast concourse of soldiers. He later recalled: "The sense of victory was in the air. The whole of North Africa was cleared of the enemy. A quarter of a million prisoners were cooped in our cages. Everyone was proud and delighted. There is no doubt people like winning very much."

But the war was far from over. Hitler's armies stood sentinel along the coastline of northern Europe, and within Europe the SS and Gestapo held down a dozen captive nations in fear and terror. The murder of six million Jews was all but completed. Churchill took a lead in issuing calls for war crimes trials once the war was won, and in warning the Germans that retribution, when it came, would be severe. But the only sure method of ending mass murder and tyranny was to defeat Germany militarily. To do this, an Allied army had to land in north-west Europe, endeavour to drive the Germans out of the lands they were occupying, and defeat them in their heartland.

In order to ensure a successful landing in north-west Europe in 1944, during the last six months of 1943 Churchill was focusing his energies and driving forward the planning machinery with great energy. As part of the grand design, General Eisenhower was chosen as Supreme Commander of the Allied Expeditionary Force. General Montgomery would command 21 Army Group. Slowly and steadily Britain and the United States were gaining the air mastery without which any landings would be impossible. Crossing the Atlantic once

more, on 9 August Churchill reached Quebec, for a conference with Roosevelt and the Joint Chiefs of Staff, at which the decision to embark on a cross-Channel landing in nine months time was finalized, and detailed preparations put in motion.

In November, Churchill went to Teheran, for the first meeting of the Big Three: himself, Roosevelt and Stalin. Churchill urged the Soviet leader to allow democratic regimes to be established in countries overrun by Germany, once they had been liberated by the Red Army. Churchill told Stalin: "We are the trustees for the peace of the world. If we fail, there will be perhaps a hundred years of chaos... There is more than merely keeping the peace. The Three Powers should guide the future of the world. I do not want to enforce any system on other nations. I ask for freedom, and for the right of all nations to develop as they like."

Stalin had other ideas, but at each of their three further meetings – in Moscow in 1944, at Yalta and at Potsdam in 1945 – Churchill was to urge the establishment of free elections everywhere, especially in Poland, for which Britain had gone to war with Germany in September 1939. Stalin said he would adhere to democratic values, but pursued a ruthless course of establishing Communist rule, and Communist regimes, wherever his army advanced.

From Teheran, where he celebrated his sixty-ninth birthday, Churchill flew to North Africa, for more conferences with Roosevelt and the Anglo-American planners, about the war in Italy – where the Allies had landed in September – the cross-Channel landings, and the continuing harsh struggle against Japan in the Far East. While at Carthage he was taken ill.

As Churchill recovered, slowly, from this second setback, his wife flew out to North Africa to be with him, as did his daughter Sarah, who sat by his bed reading him Jane Austen's *Pride and Prejudice*. Later, his son Randolph arrived, and father and son played one of their favourite games, bezique.

On 27 December, as the year came to an end, Churchill felt well enough to fly to Marrakech – one of his favourite pre-war holiday destinations – for the final lap of recuperation. On New Year's Eve, Montgomery and Eisenhower were among those who came to wish him well. That evening, as his Private Secretary Jock Colville noted, "Punch was brewed, the PM made a little speech, the clerks, typists and some of the servants appeared, and we formed a circle to sing 'Auld Lang Syne'."

LEFT Roosevelt and Churchill
give a press conference in
Casablanca, January 1943.

LEFT Churchill and Roosevelt at
Casablanca, with the two rivals
for French leadership, General
Giraud (far left) and, smoking
a cigarette, General de Gaulle.

ABOVE Churchill leaves his villa at the end of the Casablanca Conference. At his side, in army uniform, is his son Randolph, who had been serving with a special commando unit in the Western Desert, where he had been wounded. He was later to volunteer to be parachuted into German-occupied Yugoslavia. Immediately behind Churchill are his naval aide-de camp, Commander "Tommy" Thompson, and his detective, Inspector Walter Thompson. On the left of the picture, holding his coat, is John Martin, Churchill's Principal Private Secretary.

RIGHT On 30 January 1943 Churchill flew from Cairo to the southern Turkish city of Adana, where he held talks with the Turkish President, Ismet Inönü, a veteran on the Turkish side of the 1915 Gallipoli campaign. During their talks, Inönü agreed that Turkey would remain neutral, but would make facilities available to Britain. Here the two men are talking in the Turkish presidential train.

ABOVE Churchill – and cigar – at Adana, in the cockpit of the plane that flew him to Turkey and back. Turkish and Soviet emblems show where it had flown previously. This was Churchill's last flight on *Commando*. Later, with a different pilot and crew, she crashed with the loss of all on board.

ABOVE General Sir Bernard Montgomery greets Churchill
on 3 February 1943, at Castel Benito airport in Tripoli.

ABOVE Outside Tripoli, Churchill thanks the soldiers of the 8th Army, on behalf of King George VI, for their "historic advance" that had driven the German and Italian armies out of Libya and Tunisia.

ABOVE Men of the Royal Armoured Corps stand to attention as Churchill rides along the line of troops and tanks to the triumphal columns erected in Tripoli by the Italian dictator, Benito Mussolini.

LEFT Churchill crosses the Atlantic in May 1943 to meet Roosevelt. With him on board ship are the Chief of the Air Staff, Air Chief Marshal Sir Charles Portal; the First Sea Lord, Admiral of the Fleet Sir Dudley Pound and the Chief of the Imperial General Staff, General Sir Alan Brooke. On Churchill's left is General Sir Archibald Wavell, who had commanded in the Western Desert, and was soon to go to India as Viceroy.

BELOW Churchill reaches the United States, giving his "V-for-Victory" sign to Allied sailors and airmen who had crossed the Atlantic with him. Coming down the steps behind Churchill is Vice Admiral Adolphus Andrews, United States Navy Commander of the Eastern Sea Frontier of the United States. An American sailor stands guard.

LEFT On 19 May 1943, Churchill makes his second wartime address to both Houses of Congress, as well as to members of Roosevelt's Cabinet and the United States Supreme Court. Behind Churchill is Vice President Henry A. Wallace and, next to Wallace, Representative Sam Rayburn, respectively the presiding officers of the Senate and House of Representatives. In the foreground are Senators Alben W. Barkley and Charles L. McNary, leaders of the Senate majority and minority. In his speech, Churchill pledged full British support to the United States in the defeat of Japan, and stressed that the intensified Allied air bombardment of Germany was paving the way for Hitler's downfall.

LEFT Churchill and Roosevelt have a brief moment of relaxation during the Washington Conference on 24 May 1943, shortly before a group photograph (below) of the Anglo-American military, naval and air chiefs.

BELOW Planning for victory. A group photograph on the lawn of the White House, 24 May 1943. Standing, left to right, are: Field Marshal Sir John Dill, Chairman of the British Joint Staff Mission; Lieutenant General Sir Hastings Ismay, head of Churchill's Defence Office (as Chief Staff Officer); Air Chief Marshal Sir Charles Portal, Chief of the British Air Staff; General Sir Alan Brooke, Chief of the British Imperial General Staff; Admiral Sir Dudley Pound, British First Sea Lord and Chief of the Naval Staff; Admiral William D. Leahy, United States Chief of Staff to the Commander-in-Chief of the Army and Navy (President Roosevelt); General George C. Marshall, Chief of Staff of the United States Army; Admiral Ernest J. King, Commander-in-Chief of the United States Fleet and Chief of Naval Operations and Lieutenant General J.T. McNarney, Deputy Chief of Staff of the United States Army.

ABOVE Churchill greets the staff of the British Embassy and British military missions to Washington. After his "V-for-Victory" sign, he told them of the important work they were doing for the war effort, even though they were so far from Britain and the war zones.

RIGHT Churchill studies photographs taken from a Flying Fortress, showing bomb damage done during an American daylight raid over Italy. With him is General James H. Doolittle, Commanding the United States 12th Air Force and the North-West Strategic Air Forces. Churchill's daughter Sarah was working in England at photo-reconnaissance headquarters.

ABOVE Returning to North Africa, on 1 June 1943, Churchill was greeted by thousands of troops of the British 1st Army, gathered in the Roman amphitheatre in Carthage. In his speech he thanked them for their part in the victory in North Africa. The officer to his left (without hat) taking a photograph is John Profumo, later Secretary of State for War in Harold Macmillan's government. The photograph was lost with all Profumo's belongings when the ship on which he was travelling across the Mediterranean was torpedoed.

RIGHT Churchill leaving the amphitheatre with Lieutenant General Kenneth Anderson, General Officer Commanding the British 1st Army during the North African campaign. Behind Churchill is Anthony Eden.

ABOVE While in North Africa in June 1943, Churchill visited a submarine depot and thanked the officers and men of the Submarine Service for their dedicated service and contribution. He is seen here shaking hands with submarine commanders.

RIGHT While visiting British troops in Tripoli on 2 June 1943, Churchill climbed on to a German Mark VI Tiger tank, and held one of its powerful shells in his arms.

ABOVE Churchill in North Africa, 3 June 1943, examining a map as Anthony Eden (Foreign Secretary); General Sir Alan Brooke (Chief of the Imperial General Staff); Air Marshal Sir Arthur Tedder (Air Commander-in-Chief, Mediterranean Air Command); Admiral A. B. Cunningham (Commander-in-Chief, Allied Naval Forces, Mediterranean); General Sir Harold Alexander (Deputy Commander-in-Chief, Allied Forces in North Africa); General George C. Marshall (Chief of Staff of the United States Army); General Dwight D. Eisenhower (Commander-in-Chief of the Allied Forces in North Africa) and General Sir Bernard Montgomery (Commander of the 8th Army) look on.

ABOVE The Canadian Prime Minister, William Mackenzie King, Roosevelt and Churchill at the Quebec Conference, 18 August 1943.

RIGHT Travelling from Canada to the United States, Churchill had some moments of relaxation at Niagara Falls, with his daughter Mary. In the foreground is Churchill's Principal Private Secretary, John Martin. Churchill had first visited Niagara Falls in 1900, at the age of twenty-five, while on a lecture tour of the United States and Canada.

ABOVE On 6 September 1943, Churchill visited Harvard University. After receiving an Honorary Degree he addressed American Naval and Army Cadets who were then in training at the University.

BELOW Churchill, his wife Clementine (right) and their daughter Mary
return from the United States on board the battleship *Renown*. During the
journey, they watch as a destroyer comes alongside with despatches.

RIGHT Portrait of grief. On the 26 October 1943 Churchill walked in the procession to Westminster Abbey, for the funeral of Admiral of the Fleet Sir Dudley Pound, who had been his First Sea Lord at the Admiralty since the outbreak of war, and Chief of Naval Staff from the start of Churchill's premiership. On 8 October 1943, Churchill had gone to the Royal Masonic Hospital to see Pound, and, at the request of King George VI, to place in Pound's hands the insignia of the Order of Merit. Pound, the victim of two severe strokes, was unable to speak, but recognized Churchill and grasped his hand. Pound died thirteen days later, on Trafalgar Day.

ABOVE Churchill returned to the Middle East in November 1943, for a conference at Teheran with Roosevelt and Stalin. On the outward journey he visited Malta, which had been the target of intense German air bombardment for more than two years. Uniquely in the Second World War, the island had been collectively awarded the George Cross for its courage. Here Churchill walks amid the destruction of the dockland area.

LEFT Churchill is cheered by the officers and men of the Persia and Iraq Command, who formed the guard during his stay at the British Legation in Teheran. This photograph was taken on 30 November 1943, Churchill's sixty-ninth birthday. Three battalions of the Command presented him with gifts.

RIGHT Churchill addresses officers and men of the Persia and Iraq Command, in the grounds of the British Legation, Teheran.

OPPOSITE Churchill leaving the British Legation, Teheran. He is wearing a Persian lambswool hat, and his Royal Air Force Air Commodore's uniform, as Air Commodore of 615 Squadron, based at Biggin Hill, near his home at Chartwell, in Kent. Immediately behind him is his Principal Private Secretary, John Martin.

ABOVE Roosevelt and Stalin at Churchill's birthday dinner in Teheran. On the far right is Churchill's interpreter Major Birse. Stalin was five years younger than Churchill, and Roosevelt eight years younger.

ABOVE Churchill shakes Stalin's hand at the ceremony presenting a British-made Sword of State from King George VI and the People of Britain to the People of Stalingrad, in recognition of their heroic defence of their city and the defeat of the German armies besieging it. The sword is in a presentation box on a table in the foreground. Between Stalin and Churchill is Marshal Kliment Voroshilov, Chairman of the Defence Committee of the Council of People's Commissars (Minister of Defence).

LEFT While getting ready for the formal Teheran Conference photograph, Stalin shakes hands with Churchill's daughter Sarah. Behind her (his face obscured) is the Soviet Commissar for Foreign Affairs (Foreign Minister), Vyacheslav Molotov. Directly behind Roosevelt is the new American Ambassador to the Soviet Union, Averell Harriman. Immediately behind Churchill is Sir Archibald Clark Kerr, British Ambassador in Moscow, and, on the right, the Foreign Secretary, Anthony Eden.

ABOVE Churchill and Roosevelt in Cairo, November 1943, with the Chinese Nationalist leader, General Chiang Kai-shek (sitting next to Roosevelt), and Madame Chiang Kai-shek (sitting next to Churchill). Among the others in the photograph are Anthony Eden (talking to Roosevelt), the British Foreign Secretary and Harold Macmillan (then resident British Minister in Algiers: a future Prime Minister) who is directly behind Roosevelt. Averell Harriman, then United States Ambassador in Moscow, is directly behind Madame Chiang Kai-shek. On Harriman's right (behind Churchill's left shoulder, between Churchill and Madam Chiang Kai-shek) is Major Desmond Morton, one of Churchill's advisers and his confidant on intelligence matters in the interwar years – a man who was hardly ever photographed.

OVERLEAF A historic moment in North Africa on Christmas Day 1943. Churchill, who had been seriously ill with pneumonia, and had also suffered a mild heart attack, was sufficiently recovered by Christmas Day to give an informal lunch party in Carthage for the military leaders planning the Normandy landings, which had been projected for the early summer of the following year. On the left of the picture is General Eisenhower, whom Churchill and Roosevelt had chosen to be the Supreme Commander of the cross-Channel enterprise. Next to Eisenhower is General Sir Harold Alexander, who was in overall command of the British, American and Allied forces that had recently landed in Italy. Churchill is wearing a patterned dressing gown over his siren suit.

Churchill with General de Gaulle, Marrakech, 12 January 1944.

1944

THE DRIVE TO VICTORY

CHURCHILL BEGAN THE YEAR 1944 convalescing from the pneumonia and heart trouble he had suffered in Carthage at the end of 1943. Puckishly, and also courageously, he had told his daughter Sarah at the height of his illness: "If I die, don't worry – the war is won." In the New Year he flew from Tunis to Marrakech, hoping to do some painting as part of his recovery, and to raise his spirits, as painting so often did; but, as he recalled, although his painting tackle had been sent out from England, "I could not face it. I could hardly walk at all. Even tottering from the motor-car to a picnic luncheon in lovely weather amid the foothills of the Atlas was limited to eighty or a hundred yards. I passed eighteen hours out of the twenty-four prone. I never remember such extreme fatigue and weakness in body." Britain's war leader was, as he himself wrote, "utterly tired out".

The demands of the war could not be set aside. While still recovering in Marrakech, Churchill followed closely every aspect of the preparations for the Normandy landings. As part of the military and political arrangements that had to be made, he met General de Gaulle, head of the Free French forces, whose troops were to participate in the landings. The two men discussed the participation of French troops, and the setting up of a French Provisional Government once Paris was liberated.

On 14 January 1944, although not still fully recovered, Churchill returned to Britain, travelling by air from Marrakech to Gibraltar, and then on by sea. Once back, he was quickly drawn into the details of the D-Day preparations. The Normandy landings were planned as the largest amphibious assault in history. Churchill embarked on a rigorous tour of inspection of the troops all over Britain – British, Canadian and American – who were training for the cross-Channel attack. The whole of southern England, he later wrote, "became a vast military camp, filled with men, trained, instructed, and eager to come to grips with the Germans across the water." When the attack was launched, on 6 June 1944, Churchill was able to tell the House of Commons: "Nothing that equipment, science or forethought could do has been neglected."

As the Allied armies advanced, slowly and with difficulty at first, through northern France, the Soviet forces were pushing closer and closer towards Germany from the East. Stalin was determined to establish Communist regimes in as many lands as possible, and in Moscow he had been preparing Polish, Czech, Romanian, Hungarian, Bulgarian and German Communists to take charge of their countries once Russian troops had reached their respective capitals. Churchill

the Russian armies were in place, and to establish democratic regimes in these countries, made up of all the pre-war political parties. He therefore proposed a Big Three conference in Scotland. Stalin declined, saying that his doctors would not allow him to fly. Churchill then suggested that they hold the conference in Jerusalem (which was then under British mandatory rule), to which Stalin could travel by train direct from Moscow, via the Caucasus – which had been liberated from the Germans – Turkey and Syria. Again, Stalin declined. He did not want to have to agree to anything until he was in a position to flout the agreement.

When the Poles in Warsaw rose up against the Germans in August, hoping to establish a government before the arrival of the Soviets, Churchill rushed aid to the insurgents by air from British bases in southern Italy, but the distance was too great for any effective help, and Stalin, whose air force controlled several airports less than a hundred miles from Warsaw, refused to allow the British planes to land there to refuel. Churchill was angry, but impotent. Roosevelt refused to join him in a joint challenge to Stalin, fearing that it would endanger an agreement he had reached with the Soviet leader, for the use of Soviet far eastern air bases in the war against Japan.

As the Allied armies moved steadily deeper and deeper into German-occupied Europe, Churchill continued to visit the troops whenever he could: in Normandy, in liberated Paris, in Italy, and, on Christmas Day 1944, in Athens, where he intervened, under fire, to persuade the Greek Communists to suspend their attempt to seize power and to join an all-Party government.

Churchill was seventy-years-old, but his capacity for hard work was not diminished, either by past illness, long travels, or the uncertainties of what would happen to Europe – especially Eastern Europe – once Germany was defeated. If anything, the accumulation of problems seemed to stimulate and invigorate him. On the flight back from Athens, Elizabeth Layton – one of the two secretaries who was with him noted in her diary: "I went along to the tail of the plane where he was in bed and working. I sat on the typewriter box and tried not to fall off when the plane jerked, which it did quite frequently. He just worked in the usual way, me passing the ashtray every few minutes."

Churchill was back in Britain on 29 December. "You know I can't give you the excitement of Athens every day", he remarked on New Year's Day to Marian Holmes – the other secretary who had

ABOVE His convalescence at an end, Churchill returned to Britain from
North Africa in February 1944. He was met on his arrival in London by
Clementine Churchill, their daughter Diana, his granddaughter Edwina, and
members of the Cabinet, including the Chancellor of the Exchequer, Sir
John Anderson (between Mrs Churchill and her husband) and the Minister
of Production, Oliver Lyttelton (far right).

OPPOSITE Shortly after his return to Britain, Churchill visits a dockyard
where two enormous prefabricated ports (later known as Mulberry
Harbours) were being manufactured. The plan was to tow them in sections
across the English Channel, and assemble them off the coast of Normandy,
where they could enable large amounts of supplies to be brought safely
ashore after any amphibious landings. Churchill had first proposed such
artificial harbours in 1942.

OPPOSITE While inspecting American troops in Britain on 23 March 1944, Churchill fires a tommy-gun. The figure beyond Churchill, also firing, is Eisenhower.

RIGHT During an inspection by Churchill and Eisenhower of Troop Carrier Command, at a United States Army Air Force base in Britain, an American soldier loads an 81-millimetre mortar.

RIGHT Churchill, standing in an open car, talks to American troops during his visit to the United States 9th Air Force base in Britain. He told the soldiers, who were in training for the D-Day landings, that they represented "the most modern expression of war", and that their job was to batter down the "dark tyrannies which have overcrowded our lives".

LEFT Churchill inspects a Cromwell tank, one of the latest types of British Cruiser Tanks, designed for the impending battles in northern Europe. This photograph was taken on 31 March 1944, but not released by the censor until after the Normandy landings in June.

BELOW Also in March 1944, watched by his detective, Inspector Thompson, and by Lieutenant General Omar C. Bradley, Commander of the American ground forces in the Allied Expeditionary Force, Churchill inspects a bazooka, an American anti-tank weapon.

RIGHT After witnessing a mass parachute drop on British soil, Churchill addresses the American paratroopers who had participated in it. Unknown to them, the Normandy landings, in which they were to play a crucial part, were less than two-and-a-half months away.

BELOW Churchill inspects British troops on 12 May 1944.

RIGHT On 15 May 1944, during a break in his tour of inspection of British and Allied troops who would be taking part in the Normandy landings, Churchill demonstrates the zipper of his siren suit to General Eisenhower, the Supreme Commander of the cross-Channel Allied Expeditionary Force.

LEFT Churchill, still in a siren suit, with General Montgomery, Commander of 21 Army Group, photographed on 19 May 1944, less than a month before the Normandy landings.

OPPOSITE Churchill leaves Downing Street for Parliament on the morning of 6 June 1944, to announce the Allied landings in France. Behind him is one of his Private Secretaries, Leslie Rowan.

LEFT On 12 June 1944, six days after the Normandy Landings, Churchill, wearing a lifejacket, crossed the English Channel to France in a destroyer, after which he spent several hours ashore on the Normandy beachhead. On the far right is Rear Admiral William Parry, Naval Commander Force "L" in Invasion of France, who undertook the responsibility for Churchill's journey. On Churchill's right is Field Marshal Sir Alan Brooke (Chief of the Imperial General Staff) and on his left is Field Marshal Jan Smuts, the South African leader who had fought in the Boer War against the British, a war in which Churchill, as a young reporter, had been taken prisoner by the Boers.

RIGHT During Churchill's June visit to the Normandy beachhead he and those with him peer at an aircraft flying overhead. Is it friend or foe? From left to right: Lieutenant General Sir Richard O'Connor, British VIII Corps Commander, 21 Army Group (who had been a prisoner of war and was released from German captivity when Italy capitulated); Churchill; Field Marshal Smuts; General Montgomery and Field Marshal Brooke.

LEFT On 30 June 1944, as Hitler's "secret weapon", the V-1 flying bomb, was causing death and destruction in London, Churchill and his wife visited their daughter Mary's anti-aircraft battery in Kent, to watch the attempts being made to shoot the weapon down by artillery and the Royal Air Force. Mary Churchill points out a fighter in action above her battery.

RIGHT Churchill sits alone during his visit to his daughter's anti-aircraft battery.

ABOVE On 22 July 1944 Churchill returned to Normandy. In this picture, watched by Montgomery, he speaks to some of the troops who took part in the original landing.

RIGHT That same day, during a surprise visit to Caen, which had only just fallen into Allied hands, Churchill looked at the ruins of the town, which had been devastated by Allied bombardment before the final battle. With him are Lieutenant General Sir Miles Dempsey (centre) and General Montgomery (right).

ABOVE While visiting Normandy on 22 July 1944,
Churchill and Montgomery (sitting next to the driver)
cross the River Orne on "Winston Bridge", one of two
bridges built over the river by the Royal Engineers.
Sitting next to Churchill is Lieutenant General Sir Miles
Dempsey, the Commander of the British 2nd Army.

ABOVE Churchill in a light two-seater observation plane
in which he flew over the Normandy battle area.

OVERLEAF Churchill inspects the damage to the port of
Cherbourg, which was being reopened for a massive
Allied supply route. As a gesture of welcome when he
entered the port, a French docker offers to re-light his
cigar. Accompanying Churchill is an American two-star
general, Major General Cecil Moore, Chief Engineer of
the European Theater of Operations.

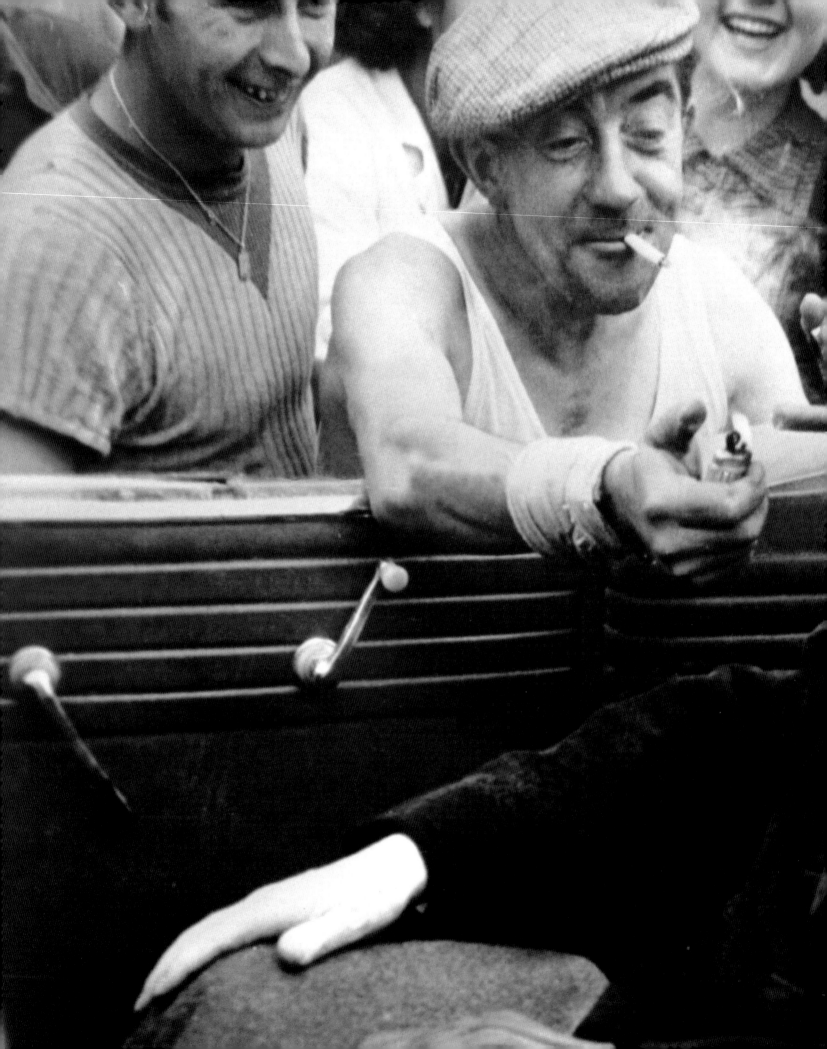

ABOVE Churchill inspects a V-1 flying-bomb launch site in the Cherbourg Peninsula, which had been overrun by the Americans before it could be put into operation.

LEFT On 7 August 1944, Churchill returned to Normandy for his third visit. Here, in Air Commodore's uniform, he strokes Rommel, General Montgomery's dog, at 21 Army Group headquarters.

BELOW Churchill with members of the crew of HMS *Kimberley* on 15 August 1944, having watched the Allied landings in the South of France. "We found ourselves," Churchill wrote to his wife later that day, "in an immense concourse of ships" and looked at "the panorama of the beautiful shore with smoke rising from many fires started by the shelling." Before the war Churchill had spent many holidays on that same coast.

ABOVE Flying to Italy, on 26 August 1944 Churchill visited a Royal Artillery battery near Florence, where he autographed one of the shells before it was fired into the German lines on a facing ridge across the valley. He then watched the battle from an observation point – next to a ruined house that had been held by the Germans only two days previously, and was within German shelling range. Its owner is sitting behind the Prime Minister and the generals. On Churchill's left is Field Marshal Alexander, Commander-in-Chief of the Allied Armies in Italy.

RIGHT As a precaution, Churchill moved into the ruined house, from where he looked across the valley through a telescope. When British shells landed in the target area, he remembered his autographed shell, and remarked: "This is rather like sending a rude letter, and being there when it arrives." Alexander later recalled: "He absolutely loved it. It fascinated him – the real warrior at heart."

LEFT Field Marshal Alexander and Churchill during a visit to British troops in Italy in August 1944. On reaching a nearby artillery battery, Churchill fired the first shot of a howitzer that had been targeted on a German artillery position north of Pisa.

LEFT While in Italy, Churchill visited the 4th Queen's Own Hussars, with whom he had served as a young officer half a century earlier. As Colonel-in-Chief of the regiment, he is wearing an army uniform as he addresses the soldiers from a jeep.

LEFT On his last wartime visit across the Atlantic, in September 1944, Churchill made a second journey to Quebec, for a conference with Roosevelt to decide the final phases of war strategy. Here Churchill stands with his wife on the platform of their railway car at Halifax, Nova Scotia, which they had reached on board the *Queen Mary*. When the crowd surged around the car, Churchill asked them to sing to him while he waited for the train to pull out. One of Churchill's secretaries, Marian Holmes, who was with him, noted: "PM stood on the observation platform and joined the crowd in singing 'God Save the King' and 'Oh Canada'. As so often on such occasions, he was deeply moved."

BELOW 11 September 1944. Churchill greets Roosevelt at Quebec. A Canadian Mountie stands guard.

ABOVE Churchill and his wife reach Greenock, in Scotland, on 26 September 1944, on their return from Quebec. Behind them is the liner *Queen Mary*, on which they had travelled.

LEFT A moment of leisure. On 3 October 1944 Churchill and his wife are among the audience at the Old Vic, in London, for a performance of George Bernard Shaw's *Arms and the Man*.

BELOW Stalin sees Churchill off from a Moscow airport, on 19 October 1944, during an inspection of a Soviet guard of honour at the end of Churchill's second visit to the Soviet Union. The two leaders held many hours of talks, during which it became clear that Stalin was determined to impose Communist control as far west as his armies could reach in their defeat of Germany and its Axis allies. Vyachelslav Molotov, who had negotiated the Nazi–Soviet Pact with Ribbentrop in August 1939 – and subsequently partitioned Poland between Germany and the Soviet Union – is on Stalin's left (in suit).

LEFT Churchill in Paris, 11 November 1944, inspecting a guard of honour of French troops, with General de Gaulle at his side.

BELOW Travelling to Paris on 11 November 1944 – the First World War Armistice Day – Churchill walks down the Champs Elysées with General de Gaulle having laid a wreath on the Tomb of the French Unknown Soldier at the Arc de Triomphe.

ABOVE Churchill and General de Gaulle inspecting General de Lattre de Tassingy's troops near Besançon on 13 November 1944.

LEFT At Christmas 1944 Churchill flew to Athens, where he presided over a conference of the warring Greek factions. Here he leaves the cruiser *Ajax*, flagship of the Eastern Mediterranean Fleet, where he was staying, to go to the British Embassy in Athens. Directly behind him on the step is his doctor, Lord Moran (formerly Sir Charles Wilson). About to leave the ship, holding some papers, and in Royal Air Force uniform, is Jock Colville, one of Churchill's Private Secretaries.

OPPOSITE Churchill reaches the British Embassy in Athens, and is helped out of the armoured control vehicle in which he had travelled from the ship amid spasmodic gunfire, as Communist Greek forces sought to overawe the capital. In the negotiations at the Embassy, Churchill persuaded the Communists to join a national Government.

Churchill, Roosevelt and Stalin — the Big Three — at the Yalta Conference.

1945
THE WAR IS WON

THE YEAR 1945 began with preparations for a meeting, in the Crimean port of Yalta, of Churchill, Stalin and Roosevelt, to discuss the future of Europe once Germany was defeated, something that was suddenly within view, possibly only a few months away. On his way to Yalta, Churchill decided to meet Roosevelt at Malta, to coordinate their policies before they met Stalin. But Roosevelt was a dying man, and was unable to play a full and constructive part in the conference.

When the Big Three gathered at Yalta, Churchill appealed to Stalin to abandon the confrontational rigidity of Communism. "Before us," he said, "lies the realization of the dream of the poor – that they shall live in peace, protected by our invincible power from aggression and evil." Stalin listened politely, even as his armies were bringing with them the imposition of Communist rule to a dozen capital cities. When Churchill asked Stalin to agree to free elections in Poland, Stalin had no hesitation in doing so, confident that when the time came – and he even offered to hold them sooner rather than later – the full apparatus of Communist control would ensure that the pre-war democratic political parties would be pushed aside.

Returning to Britain from Yalta, Churchill was soon on his travels again. On 5 March he was on German soil, crossing the Siegfried Line defences. On 24 March he was back on German soil, this time on the western bank of the Rhine, from which he watched a massive Allied paratroop drop fifteen miles east of the river. He then crossed the Rhine by amphibious vehicle, accompanied by Montgomery, who had been promoted Field Marshal seven months before. "We landed in brilliant sunshine and perfect peace on the German shore," Churchill recalled, "and walked about for half an hour or so unmolested." On the following day, he, Montgomery and Field Marshal Brooke had a picnic on the bank of the river.

On 10 April Churchill attended a memorial service at Westminster Abbey for David Lloyd George, the man who had led Britain to victory in the First World War. "There was no man so gifted, so eloquent, so forceful, who knew the life of the people so well," Churchill told the House of Commons. "When I first became Lloyd George's friend and active associate, now more than forty years ago, this deep love of people, the profound knowledge of their lives and of the undue and needless pressures under which they lived, impressed itself indelibly on my mind."

Two days after the memorial service to Lloyd George, a moment of sombre reflection for Churchill, the news was brought to him that Roosevelt was dead. "What an enviable death was his!" Churchill told the House of Commons. "He had brought his country through the worst of its perils and heaviest of its toils. Victory had cast its sure and steady beam upon him." The defeat of Germany was less than four weeks away.

Churchill sent a message of condolence on Roosevelt's death to the new President, Harry S. Truman, who replied: "At no time in our respective histories has it been more important that the intimate, solid relations which you and the late President had forged between our countries be preserved and developed." Truman and Churchill quickly discovered that they thought alike with regard to the looming Soviet danger. Even before the war with Germany was over, Churchill warned Truman – who was at one with Churchill to try to preserve Polish independence – of an "iron curtain" that had descended between the Western Allies and the Soviet Union.

On 30 April, eighteen days after Roosevelt's death, and the day after the German armies in Italy had signed terms of surrender, Hitler committed suicide deep in his underground bunker in Berlin (in 1933 Roosevelt had been inaugurated President less than five weeks after Hitler came to power). Following Hitler's death the German military resistance began to crumble, and on 7 May the German armies surrendered unconditionally. On the following day, "Victory in Europe Day", Churchill broadcast to the nation, and later that day addressed a vast crowd in Whitehall. The "evil-doers" Churchill declared in his broadcast, "are now prostrate before us." But Japan, "with all her treachery and greed, remains unsubdued".

The war against Japan continued, but despite the military needs of that distant conflict, where large numbers of British troops were in daily combat with a tenacious enemy, the Labour Party demanded an immediate return to Party politics, and a General Election was called. After the votes had been cast, but before they were counted – the delay was due to the need to bring in all the votes from those serving overseas – Churchill set off, as Prime Minister – to Potsdam, outside Berlin, for a conference of the Big Three to decide on the future of post-war Europe. At Potsdam, he met Truman for the first time as President. "I called on him the morning after our arrival," Churchill later wrote, "and was impressed with his gay, precise, sparkling manner and obvious power of decision." Like

Churchill, Truman was opposed to the Soviet view of post-war Europe, but Stalin's armies were in control of half the continent, including Poland and Czechoslovakia.

While at Potsdam, Churchill went into Berlin, where he saw the ruins of the city, and, with his daughter Mary, visited Hitler's ruined Chancellery. He also went down to the bottom of Hitler's underground bunker, and was shown the room in which Hitler and Eva Braun had committed suicide. Returning to the surface, he was shown the place where Hitler's body and that of Eva Braun had been burned.

With Churchill at Potsdam was the Leader of the Opposition, his former Deputy Prime Minister, Clement Attlee. The two men returned to Britain in mid-conference to learn the results of the General Election. The British people had turned their backs on the Conservative Party, feeling that it had let them down before the war – a feeling Churchill had done much to create during his pre-war criticisms of the Conservative government's lack of preparedness for war. The Labour Party won a landslide victory. For the first time in British history the Labour vote (almost twelve million) was higher than the Conservative vote (just short of ten million). When someone said to Churchill that the vote was a sign of the people's "ingratitude", he replied, "I wouldn't call it that. They have had a very hard time."

Churchill resigned as Prime Minister, and Attlee returned to Potsdam alone – Britain's new leader.

Churchill, in the naval uniform of an Elder of Trinity House, talks with Roosevelt at Malta on 2 February 1945, on their way to Yalta. Churchill was shocked at how ill Roosevelt looked.

ABOVE On 3 March 1945, while visiting the American 9th Army, Churchill reached the German "dragon-teeth" anti-tank fortifications of the Siegfried Line, just outside the German city of Aachen. With him are Field Marshal Sir Alan Brooke, Field Marshal Sir Bernard Montgomery, and the United States 9th Army Commander, Lieutenant General William H. Simpson.

ABOVE Churchill, Brooke, Montgomery and Simpson inspect a bridge that had been captured by the United States 9th Army.

LEFT While visiting a Canadian artillery battery on German soil, Churchill wrote a message in chalk: "A present for Hitler", and then fired the gun.

LEFT Churchill, riding in an armoured car, sees the ruins of the German town of Xanten.

RIGHT While being driven in an armoured car on conquered German soil, Churchill was wearing his army uniform as Colonel-in-Chief of the 4th Queen's Own Hussars, with whom he had served as a young officer fifty years earlier. Not long after this picture was taken, a German shell burst some fifty yards away.

LEFT On 24 March 1945, as victory draws closer, Churchill crosses the Rhine, in an American amphibious vehicle. Montgomery is on Churchill's right.

RIGHT Churchill strides ashore on the eastern bank of the Rhine. Behind him, Field Marshal Sir Alan Brooke, and behind the Field Marshal, the one female war correspondent on the crossing, Rhona Churchill (no relation to the Prime Minister).

RIGHT On the following day, 25 March 1945, Churchill, Brooke and Montgomery picnic on the west bank of the Rhine.

LEFT Churchill looks over the Rhine from a destroyed German bridge. As he did so, German shells began to fall into the river about a mile away, coming steadily closer until several fell among the motor cars that were concealed behind the bridge not far from where Churchill was standing. At that moment, the American General William H. Simpson came up to Churchill and said: "Prime Minister, there are snipers in front of you; they are shelling both sides of the bridge; and now they have started shelling the road behind you. I cannot accept responsibility for your being here and must ask you to come away." Churchill agreed. As he put his arms around the girders of the bridge for a final time, Field Marshal Sir Alan Brooke recalled how "the look on Winston's face was just like that of a small boy being called away from his sand castles on the beach by his nurse!"

ABOVE President Roosevelt died suddenly in the United States on 12 April 1945. Churchill, followed by his daughter Sarah – who worked in photographic intelligence at a Royal Air Force station in Britain – leave St Paul's Cathedral after the Memorial Service to the President on 17 April.

ABOVE May 1945: Churchill leaves Downing Street for Buckingham Palace to discuss the final arrangements for VE-Day (Victory in Europe Day) with King George VI. With him is his Private Secretary, John Peck, one of those in Churchill's inner circle who had been privy to some of the closest secrets of the war.

RIGHT On 7 May 1945, during a short break in the many telegraphic and telephone exchanges of the final day of the war in Europe, Churchill led the three Chiefs of Staff into the garden at 10 Downing Street for a group photograph. From left to right: Marshal of the Royal Air Force, Sir Charles Portal; Field Marshal Sir Alan Brooke; Churchill and Admiral of the Fleet Sir Andrew Cunningham. After the photograph was taken, Churchill, who had already put out for them a tray of drinks, raised his glass to them as "the architects of victory".

BELOW Victory in Europe Day, 8 May 1945. Churchill with the King and Queen on the balcony of Buckingham Palace.

ABOVE Churchill, returning from the Palace to Downing Street on 8 May 1945, broadcasts to the nation at three in the afternoon. The "evil-doers" he declared, "are now prostrate before us." But Japan remained "unsubdued" and must still be defeated. Churchill ended his broadcast with the words: "Advance Britannia! Long live the cause of freedom! God save the King!"

RIGHT VE-Day, 8 May 1945. On his way to the House of Commons across Horse Guards Parade, Churchill gives his "V" Sign to the crowds lining his route. Standing next to him is his detective, Inspector Walter Thompson, who had guarded him throughout the war.

ABOVE AND RIGHT VE-Day, 8 May 1945. On the balcony of the Ministry of Health, in Whitehall, Churchill greets a vast crowd celebrating the end of the war, raising his hat in recognition of their cheers. With him (above) are his War Cabinet colleagues Ernest Bevin (with glasses) and Sir John Anderson, and (right) Ernest Bevin and Oliver Lyttleton.

OPPOSITE At Potsdam, to which he had flown for the final Big Three conference of the war, Churchill shakes hands with the new President of the United States, Harry S. Truman. The two men are seen here on 16 July 1945, meeting for the first time since Truman had become President.

ABOVE On 16 July 1945, Churchill left Potsdam for Berlin, where he walked through the ruined city. With him, in uniform, is his daughter Mary.

ABOVE Berlin, 16 July 1945. Soviet soldiers look on as Churchill reaches the ruins of the Hitler's Chancellery.

LEFT Leaving the ruins of Hitler's Chancellery, Churchill gives his "V" sign to a group of British soldiers and sailor. Behind him is his daughter Mary.

RIGHT On 21 July 1945, Churchill takes the salute of British troops in Berlin. In front of him are men and tanks of the 7th Armoured Division. In the background is the Victory Column celebrating the Prussian victories over Denmark (1864), Austria (1866) and France (1870–71).

ABOVE President Truman stands between Churchill and Stalin, on 23 July 1945, during the Potsdam Conference, at the entrance to Churchill's villa. He had entertained them to dinner.

OPPOSITE Churchill returned to Britain from Potsdam on 25 July 1945, in mid-conference, in order to learn the results of the British General Election. This photograph shows him reaching Downing Street that day with Clementine. On the following day the results of the election were announced: the Conservative Party had been defeated and Churchill was no longer Prime Minister. His wartime deputy, Clement Attlee, the leader of the Labour Party, who had been with him at Potsdam as Leader of the Opposition, returned to the conference as Prime Minister. Churchill then became Leader of the Opposition – until returning as Prime Minister six years later. After four more years at Downing Street he retired in 1955. He died on 30 January 1965, at the age of ninety, honoured by a State funeral, and a memorial tablet in Westminster Abbey, inscribed "Remember Winston Churchill".

INDEX

Compiled by the author

Aachen: Churchill visits Siegfried Line near, 141
Adana (Turkey): Churchill at, 86
Aid to Russia Appeal: Clementine Churchill heads, 23, 61
aircraft: Churchill inspects, 35
Air Raid Precautions (ARP): Churchill greets workers of, 57
Ajax, HMS: Churchill leaves, 136
Alexander, General Sir Harold: with Churchill, 97, 108–9, 130, 131
Allied Expeditionary Force: Churchill inspects troops of, 115–8
Anderson, Lieutenant General Kenneth: with Churchill, 94
American Marines: Churchill inspects, 52
Anderson, Sir John: 60, 112, 150
Andrews, Vice Admiral Adolphus: with Churchill, 90
Arc de Triomphe (Paris): Churchill lays wreath at Unknown Soldier's tomb at, 135
Arctic Ocean: British aid to Russia through, 78
Argentia Bay (Newfoundland): Churchill and Roosevelt meet at, 44
Armistice Day (1944): Churchill in Paris on, 135
Armoured Control Vehicle: Churchill in, 137
Armoured Division, 7th : Churchill takes salute of, in Berlin, 155
Arms and the Man (George Bernard Shaw): Churchill in audience at, 134
Army, 8th: Churchill thanks, 88
Athens: Churchill visits (1944), 111, 136–7
Atlantic Charter: 23
Atlantic Ocean: Britain's lifeline, 7; Churchill crosses, 63, 90, 132–3
Astor, Nancy: 32
atomic bomb: 60, 83
Attlee, Clement: 23, 52–3, 60, 72; at Potsdam, 140; becomes Prime Minister, 156
Augusta (American cruiser): Churchill meets Roosevelt on, 47; steams away, 50
Australia: Churchill visits troops from, 18
Austria: a German monument to the defeat of, 155

Baku: endangered, 69
Barkley, Senator Alben W: 66, 91
Bazooka: Churchill inspects, 117
Beaverbrook, Lord: with Churchill, 45–6, 60
Belgium: invaded, 7
Beneš, President Eduard: Churchill with, 29
Berlin: Churchill visits, 140, 153, 154
Bermuda: Churchill returns to Britain through, 68
Besançon (France): Churchill inspects troops near, 136
Bevin, Ernest: 60, 150
Birmingham: Churchill visits, 57
Birse, Major: Churchill's interpreter, 105
Bismarck (German battleship): hunted down, 35
Blackie (Ship's cat, *Prince of Wales*): Churchill strokes, 51
Boche Buster HMG: Churchill inspects, 39
Boeing B17: Churchill in, 35; Churchill watches arrival of, 36
Boer War: a veteran of, with Churchill, 121

Bracken, Brendan: with Churchill, 21, 24
Bradley, Lieutenant General Omar C.: Churchill with, 117
Braun, Eva: her suicide, 140
Bricklayers' Union: Churchill a member of, 9, 71
Bristol: bombed, 23, 28
Britain: awaits German invasion, 9
British bomber offensive: against Germany, 36, 74, 91
British Expeditionary Force: evacuated, 7
Brooke, General Sir Alan: with Churchill, 74–5, 90, 92, 97, 121, 139, 141, 142, 144–5, 148
Buckingham Palace: 7, 18, 55, 147; Churchill on the balcony of, 148
Burnett, Rear Admiral Robert: with Churchill, 78

Cadogan, Sir Alexander: 47
Caen: Churchill visits, 123
Cairo: 69; conference at, 107
Camp Jackson (South Carolina): Churchill at, 72
Canada: Churchill in, 98
Canadian troops: 18, 111
Canadian Broadcasting Corporation: 67
Carthage: Churchill addresses troops at, 83, 94–5; a luncheon in, 107–8
Casablanca: Churchill and Roosevelt at, 82, 83, 84
Castel Benito (Tripoli): Churchill at, 87
Catalina seaplane: 35
Caucasus: attacked, 69
Chamberlain, Neville: replaced by Churchill, 7
Chartwell (Kent): 9, 105
Cherbourg: Churchill in, 126–7
Cherbourg Peninsula: Churchill visits, 128
Chiang Kai-shek, General: at Cairo, 107
Chiang Kai-shek, Madame: sits next to Churchill, 107
Churchill, Clementine: with her husband, 19, 21, 28, 30–31, 55, 61, 100; and aid to Russia, 23; greets her husband, 112; with her husband in Canada, 132; with her husband on his last day as Prime Minister in 1945, 157
Churchill, Mary: with her father, 62, 63, 98, 100, 122, 140, 152, 153, 155, 160
Churchill, Randolph: lands with Allied Forces, 69; with his father, 83, 85
Churchill, Rhona: and Churchill's Rhine crossing, 144
Churchill, Sarah: reads to her father, 83; works in photo-reconnaissance, 93; at Teheran, 106; with her father in Tunis, 111; with her father after Roosevelt's memorial service, 146
Churchill, Winston S.: becomes Prime Minister, 6–8;
in 1940, 7–21; inspects defences, 9–13; visits Dover and Ramsgate, 14–17; with Australian troops, 18; with the King and Queen, 18; on the Thames, 19; at a railway station, 20; inspects bomb damage, 21, 30–31;
in 1941, 22–67; on board ship, 22; with Harry Hopkins, 24; at Portsmouth, 25–27; with De Gaulle and Sikorski, 27; at Bristol, 28; with Beneš, 29; in Manchester, 30–31; in Plymouth, 32–33; inspects tanks, 34, 76–7, 96; inspects aircraft, 35; watches arrival of a Flying Fortress, 36; shooting practice, 37; works on a train, 38; inspects a heavy gun, 39; in Whitehall, 40–1; at the Mansion House, 41; watches a mock battle, 43; on board HMS *Prince of Wales*, 44–6, 51, 52; his first meeting with Roosevelt, 47–50; in Iceland, 52; with Clement

Attlee, 53; on his way to Buckingham Palace, 54; visits a Fighter Squadron, 55; visits Coventry, 56; visits Birmingham, 57; visits Liverpool, 58–9; with his War Cabinet, 60; and a photograph deception, 61; greets his daughter, Mary, 62; on board HMS *Duke of York*, 62–3; in Washington, 64–6, 92–3; in Ottawa, 66–7; in the cockpit, 68, 70;
in 1942, 69–80; inspects troops in Britain, 70, 80–1; visits a munitions factory, 71; and the Anglo-Soviet Treaty (1942), 72; watches American paratroopers, 72; visits the Soviet Union, 73–4; in the Western Desert, 74–5; greets Naval officers, 78, 96; broadcasts, 79;
in 1943, 82–110; with Roosevelt, 82, 92, 98, 105, 106, 107; at Casablanca, 84–5; in Turkey, 86; with Montgomery, 87, 119, 129; in North Africa, 88–9, 94–7; gives his "V-for-Victory" sign, 90; addresses Congress, 91; at Quebec, 98; at Niagara Falls, 98; at Harvard with American cadets, 98; on board HMS *Renown*, 100; at Admiral Pound's funeral, 101; in Malta, 102; at Teheran, 103–6; with Roosevelt and Stalin, 105, 106; at the Cairo conference, 107; with General Eisenhower, 108–9, 119; with his daughter Mary, 160
in 1944, 111–137; with General de Gaulle, 110; returns to Britain after convales-cence, 112; and the preparations for the Normandy landings, 113, 115, 117–8; at shooting practice, 114; inspects tanks, 116–7; on D-Day, 120; visits Normandy, 121, 123–5; at his daughter Mary's anti-aircraft battery, 122; visits Cherbourg, 126–8; on board HMS *Kimberley*, 129; in Italy, 130–1; returns to Quebec, 132; with Roosevelt, 132; returns from Quebec 133; visits the theatre, 134; visits Stalin, 134; in Paris, 135; inspects French troops, 136; visits Athens, 136–7;
in 1945, 138–60; with Roosevelt at Malta, 140; at Yalta, 138; on German soil, 140; crosses the Rhine, 144; picnics on the bank of the Rhine, 145; at Roosevelt's memorial service, 146; on the eve of V-E Day, 147, 148; on V-E Day, 148–151; at Potsdam, 152, 156; in Berlin, 153–5; his last day as Prime Minister, 157

Churchill tank: Churchill in, 42
Clark Kerr, Sir Archibald: 106
Cole, Representative William P, Jr.: 66
Colville, John (Jock): with Churchill, 55, 83, 136
Commando: Churchill flies in, 86
Commonwealth troops: Churchill inspects, 118
Communist regimes: in preparation, 111, 134, 139; averted, 136
Conservative Party: and Churchill's premiership, 7; British people turn their back on, 140, 156
Coventry: Churchill visits, 56
Cripps, Sir Stafford: with Churchill, 79
Cromwell tank: Churchill inspects, 116
Cunningham, Admiral of the Fleet Sir Andrew (A. B.): with Churchill, 97, 148
Czechoslovakia: Churchill inspects troops from, 29

D-Day (6 June 1944): preparations for, 111; Churchill visits troops preparing for, 115; Churchill goes to House of

Commons to announce, 149
Dempsey, Lieutenant General Sir Miles: with Churchill, 123, 124
Denmark: a German monument to the defeat of, 155
Dill, General Sir John: with Churchill, 44, 92
Divine Service: at sea, 23, 48–9
Doolittle, General James H.: with Churchill, 93
Dover: Churchill visits, 14–7
Downing Street: 7, 8, 147, 148; Churchill broadcasts from, 149; Churchill returns to, from Potsdam, 157
Duke of York, HMS: Churchill travels on, 63
Dunkirk: evacuation from, 7

Eastern Europe: its precarious future, 111
Eden, Anthony: 23, 60, 72, 97; at Teheran, 106; at the Cairo conference, 107
Edinburgh: 79
Egypt: 7, 79
Eisenhower, General Dwight D.: 83; with Churchill, 97, 108–9, 114–5, 119
El Alamein: battle of, 69, 79
Elizabeth, Queen (later Queen Mother): 18, 148
Elizabeth, Princess (later Queen Elizabeth II): 63
English Channel: Churchill watches air battle above, 16–7

Firebrace, Brigadier Roy: 72
First Lord of the Admiralty, 6
First World War: recalled, 7, 23, 43, 47, 52, 79, 135, 139
Florence: Churchill visits an artillery battery near, 130
Florida: Churchill recuperates in, 69
Flying Fortress: Churchill in, 35; Churchill watches arrival of, 36; Churchill sees photographs taken from, 93
France: invaded, 7; signs armistice, 9; start of liberation of, 149; a German monument to the defeat of, 155
Free French Forces: 111
Free Trade Hall (Manchester): Churchill visits ruins of, 31
Freeman, Air Chief Marshal Sir Wilfrid: with Churchill, 44
French Unknown Soldier: Churchill lays wreath at tomb of, 135

Gallipoli campaign (1915): 52, 86
Gaulle, General Charles de: Churchill with, 27, 84, 110, 111, 135, 136
General Election (1945): 140, 156
General Grant tank: Churchill inspects, 34–5
George VI, King: 7, 18, 47, 55, 69, 88, 101, 147, 148
George Cross: awarded to Malta, 102
Germany: and Allied war aims, 69, 83; Churchill on soil of, 139; surrenders, 139
Gestapo: 83
Gibraltar: Churchill travels through, 111
Giraud, General: Churchill with, 84
Greece: conquered, 23; Churchill's journey to, 111, 136–7
Greenock (Scotland): Churchill reaches, 133
Greenwood, Arthur: 60
Guildhall (London): bombed, 21
guns: Churchill inspects: 39

Halifax (Nova Scotia): Churchill at, 132
Harriman, Averell: with Churchill, 32–3, 63, 74; at Teheran, 106; at the Cairo

conference, 107
Harvard: Churchill addresses cadets at, 99
Henshaw, Alex: with Churchill, 58
Hill, Kathleen: with Churchill, 38, 63
Hitler: 7, 67; declares war on United States, 23; and North Africa, 69; a "present for", 142; commits suicide, 139; Churchill reaches ruins of Chancellery of, 154–5
Holland: invaded, 7
Holmes, Marian: Churchill's secretary, 111, 132
Home Fleet: Churchill visits, 78–9
Hong Kong: attacked, 63; captured 69
Hopkins, Harry: with Churchill, 24, 27, 44, 64
Horse Guards Parade (London): Churchill crosses, 149
House of Commons: unease in, 69; Churchill's assurance to, 111; Churchill on his way to, 149

Iceland: Churchill visits, 52
Inönü, Ismet: Churchill visits, 86
Ismay, Major General Hastings: with Churchill, 14, 16–17, 23, 27, 44, 92
Italian forces: in North Africa, 7, 79
Italy: 83, 93, 107; Churchill visits (1944), 111, 130–1; surrenders, 139

Japan: makes war, 23; and Allied war aims, 69, 91; and Allied war strategy, 111; still to be defeated, 139, 149
Jerusalem: a proposed Big Three conference in, 111

Kent: Churchill visits an anti-aircraft battery in, 122
Kimberley, HMS: Churchill with crew of, 129
King, Admiral Ernest J: 92
Kremlin (Moscow): Churchill in, 74

Labour Party: and Churchill's premiership, 7; and Sir Stafford Cripps, 79; and the 1945 General Election, 139, 140, 156
Lattre de Tassingy de, General: Churchill inspects troops of, 136
Layton, Elizabeth: and Churchill's return from Athens, 111
Leach, Captain: with Churchill, 44
Leahy, Admiral William D.: 92
Lend-Lease Act: "unselfish and unsordid", 23
Leslie, Lady: Churchill's letter to, 75
Liberator bomber: Churchill flies to Moscow in, 73
Libya: victory in, 88
Liverpool: Churchill visits, 58–9
Lloyd George, David: Churchill at memorial service for, 139
London: bombed, 7, 19, 21; and the V-1 flying bomb, 122
Lyttelton, Oliver: 72, 112, 150

Mackenzie King, William: with Churchill, 98
Macmillan, Harold: 94, 107
McNarney, Lieutenant General J.T.: 92
McNary, Senator Charles L: 91
Maisky, Ivan: 72
Malaya: 51, 63
Malta: Churchill visits, 102, 139; Churchill and Roosevelt at, 140
Manchester: Churchill visits, 30–1
Mansion House (London): Churchill at, 41, 160
Margesson, David: watches Churchill, 37
Marrakech: Churchill at, 83, 110
Marshall, General George C: with Churchill, 72, 92

Martin, John: with Churchill, 50, 54–5, 85, 98, 104
Ministry of Health (Whitehall): Churchill waves to the crowd from, 150–1
Molotov, Vyacheslav: 72, 106, 134
Montgomery, General Bernard: in North Africa, 69; with Churchill, 75, 87, 97, 119; to command 21 Army Group, 83; with Churchill in Normandy, 121, 123, 124, 129; with Churchill on German soil, 139, 141, 142, 144–5
Moore, Major General Cecil: with Churchill, 126–7
Moran, Lord: with Churchill, 136
Morton, Major Desmond: stands behind Churchill, 107
Moscow: Churchill's visits to, 69, 73, 83, 134
Mulberry Harbours: Churchill inspects construction of, 113
Mussolini, Benito: his triumphal columns, 89

National Liberal Club (London): Churchill on way to, 40–1
Nazi-Soviet Pact (August 1939): 134
Newfoundland: Churchill meets Roosevelt off, 23, 44–50
New Zealand: troops from, 18
Niagara Falls: Churchill visits, 98
Normandy: cross-Channel landings at, 83; preparations for, 107, 111, 112–3; Churchill visits, 111, 121, 123–5, 129
North Africa: fighting in, 7, 27, 69; Churchill's visits to, 74–5, 83, 94–7

O'Connor, Lieutenant General Sir Richard: with Churchill, 121
Old Vic Theatre (London): Churchill at, 134
Orbay, Rauf: with Churchill, 70
Order of Merit: Churchill hands insignia of to Admiral Pound, 101
Orne River: Churchill crosses, 124
Ottawa: Churchill visits, 66–7, 69

Paget, General Sir Bernard: with Churchill, 81
Paris: Churchill visits (1944), 111, 135
Parry, Rear Admiral William: with Churchill, 121
Pearl Harbor: Japan attacks, 23, 63
Peck, John: at Churchill's side, 147
Persia and Iraq Command: Churchill addresses men of, 103
Pétain, Marshal Philippe: 27
Pisa: Churchill fires a howitzer shot at a German artillery position near, 131
Plymouth: Churchill visits, 32–3
Poland: and Allied war aims, 83; and the Warsaw uprising, 111; and the Nazi-Soviet Pact, 134; and the Yalta conference, 139
Portal, Air Chief Marshal Sir Charles: with Churchill, 90, 92, 148
Portsmouth: Churchill visits, 24–7
Potsdam: conference at, 83, 139–40
Pound, Admiral of the Fleet Sir Dudley: with Churchill, 44, 90, 92; Churchill at funeral of, 101
Pride and Prejudice (Jane Austen): 83
Prime Minister: Churchill becomes, 6–8
Prince of Wales, HMS: Churchill on board, 44–6, 48–9, 50–1, 52; sunk, 69
Profumo, John: photographs Churchill, 94

Quebec: conferences at, 83, 98, 132
Queen Mary, SS: Churchill sails on, 132
Queen's Own Hussars: Churchill visits troops of, 131; Churchill in uniform of, 143

Ramsay, Vice Admiral Sir Bertram: with Churchill at Dover, 15
Ramsgate: Churchill visits, 14
Rayburn, Representative Sam: 91
"Remember Winston Churchill": 156
Renown, HMS: Churchill travels on, 100
Repulse, HMS: sunk, 69
Rhine River: Churchill crosses, 139, 144; Churchill picnics on bank of, 145
Ribbentrop, Joachim: and the Nazi-Soviet Pact, 134
Rogers, Commander Kelly: pilot to Churchill, 68
Rommel, Erwin, the "Desert Fox": 69
Rommel (Montgomery's dog): Churchill strokes, 129
Roosevelt, Eleanor: and Churchill's "siren suit", 65
Roosevelt, Elliott: with his father, 47
Roosevelt, President Franklin Delano: 7, 23; Churchill meets, 23, 47–50, 63–5, 69, 72, 83; at Casablanca, 84; Churchill on way to, 90; Churchill with (in 1943), 92, 98, 105; Churchill with (1944), 132; at Malta, 140; at Yalta, 138, 139; dies, 139, 146
Rowan, Leslie: with Churchill, 120
Royal Armoured Corps: Churchill inspects, 89
Royal Masonic Hospital: Churchill visits the dying Admiral Pound at, 101
Royal Navy: Churchill with officers of, 78, 96
Royal Tank Regiment: Churchill wears beret of, 42

St Andrews (Scotland): Churchill at, 20–1
St Paul's Cathedral (London): Churchill at Roosevelt's memorial service in, 146
Sandys, Diana (Diana Churchill): greets her father, 112
Sandys, Duncan: with Churchill, 14, 18
Sandys, Edwina: with her grandfather, 112
School of Infantry Training: Churchill visits, 81
Scotland: Churchill in, 20, 23; a proposed Big Three conference in, 111
Second Front: Stalin demands, 69, 74
Sicily: 83
Siegfried Line: Churchill at, 139, 141
Sikorski, General Wladyslaw: with Churchill, 27
Simpson, Lieutenant General William H.: with Churchill on German soil, 141, 142, 145
Sims, Admiral: a gift from, 43
Singapore: captured, 69
"siren suit": Churchill in, 64–5, 119
Smith, George: with Churchill, 24–5
Smuts, Field Marshal Jan: with Churchill, 121
South Coast (of England): Churchill inspects defences of, 9–13
South of France: Allied landings in, 129
Southampton: Churchill visits, 24
Southern Command: Churchill visits, 43, 70
Southern Rhodesian troops: 118
Soviet Union: British aid for, 23, 61, 69, 73, 78; treaty with, 72; Churchill visits, 73
Spitfire (British fighter plane): 56, 58
Stalin, Joseph: and Allied war strategy, 69; Churchill visits, 73–4; at Teheran, 83, 105, 106; his war aims, 111; Churchill's second visit to, 134; at Yalta, 138, 139; at Potsdam, 156
Stalingrad: a gift to the people of, 106
Stimson, Henry: with Churchill, 72
Stoddart, Grace: presents Churchill with a

cigar, 71
Suez Canal: 7
Syria: 111

tanks: Churchill inspects, 34, 42, 76–7, 96, 116–7
Tedder, Air Marshal Sir Arthur: with Churchill, 97
Teheran: 69, 83; Churchill at, 103–6
Thames River: Churchill travels down, 19
Thompson, Lieutenant Commander CR (Tommy): with Churchill, 52, 85
Thompson, Inspector Walter: with Churchill, 28, 37, 39, 54–5, 117, 149
Tiger tank: Churchill inspects, 96
Tobruk: overrun, 69
Tovey, Admiral John: with Churchill, 22, 79
Trafalgar Day (1943): Admiral Pound dies on, 101
Trinity House: Churchill an Elder of, 140
Tripoli: Churchill in, 87–9, 96
Troop Carrier Command (United States): Churchill inspects, 115
Truman, President Harry S.: and Churchill, 139–40; with Churchill at Potsdam, 152, 156
Tunisia: fighting in, 69; victory in, 88
Turkey: neutral, 70; Churchill visits, 86; a proposed journey through, 111

U-boats: wreak havoc, 23
United States: supplies Britain, 23, 32, 35, 36; Churchill visits 23, 61; enters the war, 69; Churchill returns to, 72, 83; Churchill inspects troops from, 115
United States Congress: Churchill addresses, 66

V-for-Victory sign: 52, 90, 93, 148, 149; in Berlin, 155
V-1 (flying bomb): Churchill watches interception of, 122; Churchill visits launching site of, 128
VE-Day (Victory in Europe Day): 139, 147; Churchill's broadcast on, 149; celebrations on, 150–1
Voroshilov, Marshal Kliment: 106

Wallace, Vice President Henry A: 66, 91
War Cabinet, 6, 8, 60
war crimes: 83
Warsaw: uprising in (August 1944), 111
Wavell, General Sir Archibald: 90
Washington DC: Churchill in, 64–6, 83, 92–3
Wellington bomber: Churchill inspects crew of, 35
Western Desert (North Africa): fighting in, 69, 74; Churchill visits troops in, 74–5; victory in, 79
Westminster Abbey (London): Churchill at memorial service in, 139; a memorial tablet to Churchill in, 156
White House (Washington): Churchill at, 65, 69, 92
Whitehall (London): Churchill in, 40–1; Churchill speaks in, 139; Churchill greets a vast crowd in, 150–1
Winant, Gilbert: with Churchill, 28
Winston Bridge: Churchill crosses, 124
Wood, Sir Kingsley: 60

Xanten (Germany): Churchill sees ruins of, 143

Yalta: conference at, 83, 138, 139
Yugoslavia: conquered, 23; Randolph Churchill parachuted into, 85

PICTURE CREDITS

All the photographs reproduced in the book have been taken from the collections of the Photograph Archive at the Imperial War Museum. The Museum's reference numbers for each of the photographs are listed below, giving the page on which they appear in the book and any location indicator (t-top, b-bottom, l-left, r-right, c-centre)

CHAPTER 1

6	HU83283
8	HU73115
9t	H2269
9m	H2270
9b	H2272
10-11	H2834
12-13	H2628
14t	H3514
14b	H3517
15	H3508
16	H3499
17	H3504
18t	H3718
18b	PL10757
19t	H4367
19b	H4365
20	H4985
21t	HU63613
21b	HU63616

CHAPTER 2

22	HU87992
24	KY879A
25	H6946
26-27	H6945
27	H7233
28t	H8863
28-29b	HU60902
29t	HU90343
30t	KY442007
30b	HU61398
31	HU63614
32	H9265
33	H9267
34	H9913
35t	H10298
35b	H10305
36	H10313
37	H10688
38	H10874
39	H10868
40-41	HU86053
41r	HU90344
42	H9922
43	H12041
44t	A4859
44b	H12799
45	A4862
46	H12776
47	H12719
48-49	A4811
50t	A4816
50b	H12752
51	H12756
52t	A4970
52b	H12862
53	HU90346
54	HU90347
55t	H14201
55b	H14198
56t	H14250
56b	H14259
57	H14260
58t	H14264
58b	H14266
59	H14265
60	CP8705
61	H16020

62	H16479
63	A6905
64	A6919
65t	A6920
65b	A6921
66t	NYP54878
66b	A6720
67t	H16429
67b	CAN578

CHAPTER 3

68	H16632
70t	H16637
70b	H18190
71tr	H18481
71bl	H19756
71br	H19751
72t	CH5711
72b	HU90421
73t	FLM1116
73b	FLM1114
74t	RR1077
74b	E15907
75	E15391
76-77	H18498
78t	H24535
78b	A12156
79t	A12151
79b	H20446
80	H25441
	H25955

CHAPTER 4

82	NA481
84t	A14062
84b	NY6082
85	A14155
86t	K3987
86b	K4473
87	E22240
88	E22258
89	E22277
90t	A16709
90b	A16710
91	NY7793
92t	HU90349
92b	HU90350
93t	HU90348
93b	CNA854
94l	CNA846
94-95	NA3253
96t	A17038
96b	NA3277
97	NA3286
98t	H32129
98b	H31943
99	H32728
100	H32947
101	HU90345
102	A20581
103t	A20747
103b	A20746
104	A20723
105	A20732
106t	E26631
106b	A20714
107	TC10203
	NA10074

CHAPTER 5

110	HU60057
112	HU90351
113	P1771
114	H36960
115t	EA18275
115b	EA18357
116-117	H37169
117r	EA18482
118r	HU90247
118b	H38443
119t	H38458
119b	H38661
120	PL25580
121t	B5354
121b	B5364
122t	H39488
122b	H39498
123t	B7888
123b	B7881
124	B7873
125	HU61431
126-127	OWIL30645
128	HU90422
129t	B8766
129b	A25247
130t	NA18044
130b	NA17912
131t	NA17872
131b	NA18017
132t	H40051
132b	H40057
133	H40335
134t	HU90352
134b	HU90354
135t	HU90423
135b	HU90353
136t	HU90424
136b	A26925
	NAM158

CHAPTER 6

138	MOI52172
140	EA52870
141	HU90425
142t	EA56602
142b	B15220
143t	BU2268
143b	BU2272
144t	BU2248
144b	BU2249
145t	BU2636
145b	EA59831
146	HU90355
147	HU90426
148t	H41824
148b	HU56527
149t	H41844
149b	CP68814
150l	HU62377
150-151	MOI68779
152	BU8944
153	BU8957
154	BU8950
155t	BU8962
155b	BU9078
156	BU9197
157	HU90356
160	HU90428

Churchill at the Mansion House, waving at onlookers, on 30 June 1943. With him is his daughter Mary. He had just been made a Freeman of the City of London. The ceremony had taken place at the Guildhall; the luncheon was held at the Mansion House. The brick wall on the left was part of the Mansion House's wartime emergency entrance.

AUTHOR'S ACKNOWLEDGEMENTS

I am grateful to Caradoc King and Martha Lishawa of the literary agency A.P. Watt, for enabling this project to go ahead; to Terry Charman of the Imperial War Museum for providing me with a mass of photographs from which to choose the pictures in this book and also for giving me the benefit of his considerable expertise in the military, naval and air spheres; to my friend Max Arthur for his wise advice on layout and content; to Juliet Solomon for her help and encouragement; to my son David for essential computer guidance, and to Kay Thomson for her logistical support.